MUSIC IN
CATHOLIC WORSHIP
The Bishops' Committee on the Liturgy

THE NPM COMMENTARY
A Collection of Articles First Published in
Pastoral Music Magazine

Edited by
Rev. Virgil C. Funk

The Pastoral Press
National Association of Pastoral Musicians
Washington, D.C.

First Printing   January, 1982
Revised Edition July, 1983
Third Printing   July, 1984

Articles in this publication first appeared in Pastoral Music, copyrighted 1977, 1978, 1979, 1980.

ISBN 0-9602378-4-4   All rights reserved.
© The National Association of Pastoral Musicians 1982, 1983.
The Pastoral Press
National Association of Pastoral Musicians
225 Sheridan Street NW, Washington, DC 20011
(202) 723-5800

CONTENTS

INTRODUCTION

In 1972, the Bishops' Committee on the Liturgy, a standing committee of the National Conference of Catholic Bishops in the United States, issued a series of guidelines for the liturgical renewal, Music in Catholic Worship. No one at the time realized just how important this document was to be for the American Church. Its clear, jargon-free language is a model of brevity and clarity. Because it was originally written in English (as opposed to documents translated from Latin) both its ideas and their expression are thoroughly American. This alone should motivate the liturgical community to continue its vigorous pursuit of cultural adaptation in North America. Music in Catholic Worship has come to be, not simply because of its authoritative source, but because of its clarity of expression and the straightforwardness of its directives, the classic document in American liturgical renewal.

In 1976, the National Association of Pastoral Musicians, an association of musicians and clergy dedicated to fostering the art of liturgical music, began a series of commentaries on sections of the document in its membership journal, Pastoral Music. These commentaries extended over a four year period. The finest liturgists and musicians in the United States—authors recognized for liturgical scholarship, musicianship and pastoral practice—were invited to address the document from three points of view: Based on parish level experience, 1) What does the document recommend that is desirable and that we have carried out? 2) What have we not done? and 3) What does the document say that needs to be revised? This book is the result of the requests of NPM members to bring the commentaries into one volume.

The complete text of Music in Catholic Worship is divided into six major sections: The Theology of Celebration, Pastoral Planning for Celebration, The Place of Music in the Celebration, General Considerations on Liturgical Structure, Application of the Principles of Celebration to Music in Eucharistic Worship, and Music in Sacramental Celebrations. The order of this book follows that outline, combining the General Considerations on Liturgical Structure and Application of the Principles of Celebration to Music in Eucharistic Worship into one section.

The first edition of this commentary was issued in 1982, the tenth anniversary of *Music In Catholic Worship*. In January, 1983, the Bishops' Committee on the Liturgy issued a new edition of that document, edited for grammatical and typographical errors and noninclusive language, but containing no substantive changes. The 1983 revision is contained in this book. We urge every person connected with liturgy—the musicians, the clergy, the planners, the ministers, and even the members of the assembly—to read, mark, and digest this document. It is a classic.

Rev. Virgil C. Funk
July 1, 1983

MUSIC IN
CATHOLIC WORSHIP

The Bishops' Committee on the Liturgy

THE NPM COMMENTARY

A Collection of Articles First Published in

Pastoral Music Magazine

FOREWORD
to the Second Edition (1983)

On December 4, 1983, the Church will mark the twentieth anniversary of the promulgation of the *Constitution on the Sacred Liturgy* of the Second Vatican Council. That event will be best commemorated by a careful restudy of the principles and norms for the restoration and promotion of the liturgy contained within the conciliar constitution and the subsequent decrees and instructions of the Holy See. Additional reflection upon the increasingly healthy state of the Church's liturgical life will confirm the Council Fathers' farsightedness in calling for liturgical reform.

Music in Catholic Worship, a statement of the Bishops' Committee on the Liturgy which was published in July 1972, has greatly assisted that renewal of the liturgy, particularly within the Church in the United States. Its clear principles have contributed to a steady improvement in the Church's liturgy, in which liturgical music serves as a necessary and integral component.

With the recent publication of *Liturgical Music Today* (1982), a decision was made to publish a revised tenth anniversary edition of *Music in Catholic Worship.* No substantive changes have been made in the revised text; what has been removed are typographical mistakes, noninclusive language and a few grammatical errors which found their way into the first edition. A new format has been provided to make *Music in Catholic Worship* a worthy companion to *Liturgical Music Today.*

I am pleased to introduce this second edition of *Music in Catholic Worship.* I am confident that its impact on good liturgical celebration will continue to be felt for many years to come.

December 1, 1982   Bishop John S. Cummins
                                   Chairman
                                   Bishops' Committee on the Liturgy

Music in Catholic Worship

INTRODUCTION
to the First Edition (1972)

In November 1967, the Bishops' Committee on the Liturgy published a statement on music entitled "The Place of Music in Eucharistic Celebrations." It had been drawn up after study by the then Music Advisory Board and submitted to the Bishops' Committee on the Liturgy, which approved the statement, adopted it as its own, and recommended it for consideration by all. The following statement on music in liturgical celebrations is a further development of that statement and was drawn up after study by the committee on music of the National Federation of Diocesan Liturgical Commissions. Their work was reviewed by the Bishops' Committee on the Liturgy and their advisors. The finished document is presented to all by the Bishops' Committee on the Liturgy as background and guidelines for the proper role of music within the liturgy.

In the course of this century, music and its role in the liturgy have been the subject of many documents. On November 22, 1903, the motu proprio *Tra le Sollecitudini* of Saint Pius X was promulgated; on December 20, 1928, the apostolic constitution of Pope Pius XI, *Divini cultus,* was published; the encyclical of Pope Pius XII, *Musicae sacrae disciplina,* was promulgated on December 25, 1955. On September 3, 1958, the Congregation of Rites issued an instruction on sacred music and the sacred liturgy. The crescendo of documents, both major and minor, on the role of music in liturgy continued and reached the culminating point in Vatican II's Constitution on the Liturgy which gave an entire chapter to sacred music. The liturgical constitution explained the role of music in divine services and formulated a number of principles and guidelines.

The latter prompted the 1967 statement of the Bishops' Committee on the Liturgy. With the lapse of time since then, the pastoral situation in the United States can be regarded with greater calm and serenity. However, it is urgent that fresh guidelines be given to foster interest with regard to music in the liturgy.

Experience with the 1967 statement makes it clear that mere

observance of a pattern or rule of sung liturgy will not create a living and authentic celebration of worship in Christian congregations. That is the reason statements such as this must take the form of recommendation and attempts at guidance. In turn, this demands responsible study and choice by priests and leaders of singing: "A very wide field of diverse liturgical practice is now open, within the limits set by the present discipline and regulations...Not all priests appreciate how wide the opportunities are for planning lively and intelligible celebration" (National Conference of Catholic Bishops, April 1967)—especially in the various combinations of song and spoken prayer in the liturgy.

It is hoped that this statement of the Bishops' Committee on the Liturgy will be of use to the bishops and their liturgical commissions and to all who celebrate or plan liturgies.

Music in Catholic Worship: Section I

THE THEOLOGY OF CELEBRATION

THE THEOLOGY OF CELEBRATION

1. We are Christians because through the Christian community we have met Jesus Christ, heard his word in invitation, and responded to him in faith. We gather at Mass that we may hear and express our faith again in this assembly and, by expressing it, renew and deepen it.

2. We do not come to meet Christ as if he were absent from the rest of our lives. We come together to deepen our awareness of, and commitment to, the action of his Spirit in the whole of our lives at every moment. We come together to acknowledge the love of God poured out among us in the work of the Spirit, to stand in awe and praise.

3. We are celebrating when we involve ourselves meaningfully in the thoughts, words, songs, and gestures of the worshipping community—when everything we do is wholehearted and authentic for us—when we mean the words and want to do what is done.

4. People in love make signs of love, not only to express their love but also to deepen it. Love never expressed dies. Christians' love for Christ and for each other, Christians' faith in Christ and in one another must be expressed in the signs and symbols of celebration or they will die.

5. Celebrations need not fail, even on a particular Sunday when our feelings do not match the invitation of Christ and his Church to worship. Faith does not always permeate our feelings. But the signs and symbols of worship can give bodily expression to faith as we celebrate. Our own faith is stimulated. We become one with others whose faith is similarly expressed. We rise above our own feelings to respond to God in prayer.

6. Faith grows when it is well expressed in celebration. Good celebrations foster and nourish faith. Poor celebrations weaken and destroy it.

7. To celebrate the liturgy means to do the action or perform the sign in such a way that the full meaning and impact shine forth in clear and compelling fashion. Since these signs are vehicles of communication and instruments of faith, they must be simple and comprehensible. Since they are directed to fellow human beings, they must be humanly attractive. They must be meaningful and appealing to the body of worshippers or they will fail to stir up faith and people will fail to worship the Father.

8. The signs of celebration should be short, clear and unencumbered by useless repetition; they should be "within the people's power of comprehension and normally should not require much explanation."[1]

If the signs need explanation to communicate faith, they will often be watched instead of celebrated.

9. In true celebration each sign or sacramental action will be invested with the personal and prayerful faith, care, attention, and enthusiasm of those who carry it out.

Theology of Celebration

BY AIDAN KAVANAGH

Fr. Kavanagh, OSB, Professor of Liturgics at the Divinity School of Yale University, is a monk of St. Meinrad Archabbey, Associate Editor of Worship *and* Studia Liturgica, *and founder of the Murphy Center for Liturgical Research at the University of Notre Dame.*

Rivers are bodies of water that move from place to place. While this movement may not always be immediately perceptible, it is constant. Should movement cease altogether, river becomes swamp, and the organisms that feed on death take over with relentless vigor.

The liturgy is like a river. At certain places, in certain times, it runs fast, clear, deep and alive; at others, sluggish, muddy, shallow and stagnant. We measure vitality by visual reference to fixed points: a tree or rock for a river, a text or artifact for the liturgy. While such reference points are not the life of a river or a liturgy, they do help us gauge the vitality of each.

Music in Catholic Worship, issued in 1972, is a case in point. Revisiting it after ten years may give us some notion of how both the liturgy and we have changed. This knowledge cannot be inert, for what it really tells us is what the liturgy and we who celebrate it are in the present.

Ten years is not a very significant span of time for the liturgy, but it is indeed a considerable period for me—one-sixth of my life. Allow me thus to reflect on how I read the document's first part, "The Theology of Celebration," ten years after it first appeared, understanding as you read this that I have changed more, perhaps, in the past ten years than has the liturgy.

First, the title is misleading. What this initial section offers is not *the* but *a* theology of celebration. More precisely, there seem to be two theologies of celebration encased in this section, neither of

5

which is fully worked out or wholly reconciled to the other.

One theology is based on a modern philosophy of personalism and may be detected in the affective words and phrases of paragraphs 1–4 and 9 ("hear and express," "renew and deepen"; "to deepen our awareness of, and commitment to. . ."; "meaningfully," "wholehearted and authentic for us"; "personal and prayerful faith, care, attention and enthusiasm").

The other theology is based on a more objective notion of the social nature of sacrament and liturgy. Paragraph 7 states: "To celebrate the liturgy means to do the action or perform the sign. . ." "To do the action" is the strongest objective statement in this section. But it is immediately qualified by being made apparently synonymous with "perform the sign," a scholastic phrase foreign to modern usage, which then leads into another affective, personalist statement, ". . . in such a way that the full meaning and impact [or the action-sign] shine forth in clear and compelling fashion." A certain objectivity may also be detected in paragraph 5, but it is muted by being made an awkward caution against too much emphasis on "feelings."

In sum, one might say that the section encases both personalist-affective and social-objective theologies of celebration, each of which is exploitable independently of the other but are here rather juxtaposed, the latter being qualified by the former.

This was an accurate reflection of the state of the question ten years ago, and I suspect it is the opinion generally shared by most people today. The liturgy surely shows its effects: it has become didactically verbose and preoccupied with generating a cogent experience for a whole range of special interest groups, becoming more an educational than a ritual event. Texts increasingly displace images, and a creeping impatience with ambiguity visits on liturgical space, things, music and ceremony a certain iconoclasm that may promise more clarity concerning the affairs of God and humankind than can be delivered. We talk much about how to prepare children for celebration, as though celebration were a commodity absent from children's lives in the first place; as though a farmer needs a course in agriculture to celebrate the harvest festival.

What results is to heat up the liturgy as a medium of communication, making it a teaching device one must do homework to understand rather than a profoundly human institution that inevitably occurs in some form whenever people assemble for a common purpose. In the latter circumstance one discovers a vast roominess and rich ambiguity that seduces all into active participation (as does a football game or Thanksgiving dinner). In the former circumstance, one discovers a narrow and brittle rationalism that both tires its audience and reduces participation to passive receptivity. The Unknown is explained, often with palpable condescension, to the unknowing, and the reality of Christian existence is thus not so much secularized as trivialized in the process. It is this notion of celebration, apparently, that the document chooses to emphasize.

This may go far to explain why our liturgical celebrations often fall short of our expectations. We promise people a party and then give them a more or less deritualized event of religious education in this or that. The germs of this attitude, it must be admitted, already lie embedded in the *Constitution on the Sacred Liturgy*, which shows some naivete concerning the nature of rite itself when it states in its paragraph 34 that "The rites . . . should be short, clear, and unencumbered by useless repetition; they should be within the people's powers of comprehension and normally should not require much explanation." The statement appears again in paragraph 8 of *Music in Catholic Worship*. The fact is that rituals are almost never short, clear and without repetition; nor do they always fall within everyone's power of comprehension (as a classroom lecture must) when they are concerned with matters of *divine* service.

Many Protestant denominations have journeyed down the road of worship-as-education for four centuries. It is paradoxical that just as some of them have begun to rediscover the participatory power of true ritual, Roman Catholics have embraced what these Protestants have discovered from much experience does not work.

The mistake is not a minor one. It seems to involve the assumption that once one has said that sacraments are about meaning there is nothing more to say. This is not true. Sacraments are about *human* meaning, a qualification that rises to the first rank among theological assertions when one deals with a faith resting on incarnational foundations. If human nature has been invested, so to speak, with divinity in the incarnation of Jesus Christ, then human meaning must equally have been thrown open to the abiding presence of divine resonances no ear has heard nor eye beheld. Human effort to verbalize this whole theandric sweep of meaning in short, clear and unrepetitious assertions or ritual acts is simply not possible. One doubts it is even possible when human meaning alone is concerned, as poets and musicians surely know.

Equal reserve needs to be used in dealing with the often unexpressed assumption that since the liturgy and the sacraments, like the Sabbath, are for us rather than we for them, they are therefore ours to dispose of as we will. This is also not true. While whole cultures do form their own idioms of faith, including liturgical systems, these idioms and systems remain accountable to the Word enfleshed; they may not run counter either to revelation or to the nature with which the Creator has endowed humankind. These are givens, implacable necessaries about which faith and worship must always be measured. In this view, while the liturgy is for us, it is for us not as a plaything but as a standard of fidelity to what we have become by the divine pleasure in Christ. Rather than "celebrating" the liturgy, perhaps it is more accurate to speak, as the Byzantine tradition does, of "serving" the liturgy, since its very core is of divine endowment upon us ("Do this as my *anamnesis*") rather than something produced wholly out of our own resources.

It is for these reasons that I would urge readers of the first nine paragraphs of *Music in Catholic Worship* to give primary weight to the fundamental statement (even though it appears only in paragraph 7) that *to celebrate the liturgy means to do the action or perform the sign*. All else is subordinate to this, and paragraph 8 is simply a well-meant inaccuracy.

COMMENTARY ON 1–2

Boring, Isn't It?

BY FRANK NORRIS

Fr. Norris is Associate Director of the Institute for Continuing Education, sponsored jointly by the Society of St. Sulpice and the Jesuit School of Theology at Berkeley, California. He was formerly a member of the Board of Directors of the Liturgical Conference.

Liturgical celebration is not meant to bring about or "create" faith in the individual or in the community as a whole. The young pre-Christian Augustine may indeed have been moved by the sight and especially the sound of the Liturgy of the Word at the cathedral church in Milan, but the experience, of itself, was not enough to bring him to embrace Christianity. At most it was a modest link in a long chain of events that contributed to his surrender to the Lord and to the consolation and the demands of the Gospel.

Liturgical celebration presupposes an existing faith community, an assembly of women and men who have already undergone conversion and who are open to the continuing process of reconversion that is at the heart of the Christian life. This is a point that should in theory need no belaboring. In actual fact it is far from being universally or perhaps even commonly grasped. Some years ago a friend, a teaching sister in a parochial school, generously volunteered to spend time on Saturdays with a group of boys and girls of high school age who were almost all dropouts from regular church attendance. "Boring" was the word they used repeatedly to describe their experience of the Mass. My friend thought that if they were to take part in a celebration that actively involved them and that was geared more to their level of understanding, they might see the Mass in a new and more positive light.

She and her young companions set about preparing for "their Mass" for more than two months. They chose readings that appealed to them, music suited to their tastes, the "right" young priest, who agreed to celebrate the Eucharist with them on a quiet beach in the late afternoon as the sun was setting over the Pacific. They themselves made the bread, the plate and the cup for the celebration, the simple table and the vestments the celebrant would wear. When at last it took place the actual celebration was to all appearances an unqualified "success." The feedback that the sister later received from the group was exuberant in its enthusiasm. "If Mass were like that all the time I'd never miss." "Why can't all priests be like Father Bob?" "That was the most moving experience of my life."

One of the young persons, however, expressed her reaction to the Mass on the beach with a bit more precision, and in so doing probably voiced the sentiments of others in the group. The music, the sense of fellowship, the beauty of the setting and warmth of the celebrant all evoked the highest praise from her. But, she concluded, "I liked everything about the Mass, Sister, except that boring part in the middle—you know, that prayer where the priest says, 'On the night he was betrayed'. . . ."

We sometimes expect too much of the Mass. In the years prior to the liturgical changes of the past decades many of us who were pressing for those very changes probably entertained unrealistic and naive notions about the results a reformed and revitalized liturgy would surely effect in the lives of Catholics generally. Certainly few of us anticipated the present state of affairs, one that is by no means totally negative, to be sure, but one that is far from a realization of our dreams of ten and fifteen years ago. Doubtless disaffection from the Church (expressed, in part, by decreased Mass attendance) is, in its causes, a complex and not a simple phenomenon. Andrew Greeley, for example, sees the Church's stand on birth control as the primary reason for the departure of many Catholics from active Church life. However that may be, it should be apparent to all that the liturgical celebration, however well prepared and carried out, has not in and of itself renewed and revitalized parish life in this country. Liturgy presupposes a community of faith.

All of which corroborates, in my view, Juan Segundo's thesis that the crisis facing the Church today is not a liturgical crisis; it is a crisis of community. The liturgy is not meant to be an isolated moment of grace but rather a recapitulating moment. Liturgical celebration—the Sunday Eucharist par excellence—should be the moment when the believing community gathers to bring into focus, to celebrate, and, by the power of the Spirit, to deepen *its commitment as a community to be the Body of Christ in the world.* Therefore if there is not a faith-inspired struggle on the part of the local church to engage in the work of healing, reconciliation and liberation that is demanded by the conditions under which all humanity lives in one form or another, then there is little or nothing to recapitulate and to be deepened at liturgy. *No authentic community, no authentic liturgy.* To believe or act otherwise is, like it or not, to make liturgy at best an aesthetically pleasurable experience removed from the reality of human existence, and at worst, a species of magic. Liturgy, once again, presupposes for its "validity" a faith community actively engaged in the tasks of healing and reconciling love that are the core of the Church's mission.

This is not to say that those concerned with the excellence of liturgical celebration are wasting their time. The urgent reality of the crisis of community does not, in my opinion, render of little account the efforts of those who—at both the theoretical and the practical level—endeavor to renew and revitalize worship in our churches, to make liturgical celebrations the finest, the most appealing and the most challenging signs (for that is what they are meant to be) of the Paschal Mystery of the Lord and of our incorporation into it. My only reason for dwelling on the need for a faith community as a presupposition of liturgical celebration is my conviction that heightened consciousness of this need is absolutely necessary if we are to understand in perspective and evaluate correctly our roles as liturgical ministers of whatever sort. Articles 1 and 2 of "The Theology of Celebration" (*Music in Catholic Worship*) might profitably be expanded to spell out explicitly the relation between the community of faith and liturgical celebration.

Although liturgy is not intended of itself to bring about initial conversion to the Lord Jesus, it surely is meant to be the occasion for reconversion, a deepening of the commitment of the local church to be a Christian community, an incarnation and epiphany of Christ's redemptive love in this world. Whatever those who plan liturgical celebrations and assume roles of leadership at liturgy can do to enhance the act of worship and make it a "better sign" is important. What follows are some general considerations—presented by one who admittedly is not a church musician —as to how those who plan and lead in liturgical celebrations, including musicians, should, in light of the theological observations presented, go about their task.

Good liturgies are integrated in their various parts. They present a clear and unified central message: an aspect of the Paschal Mystery to be proclaimed and responded to in faith and to be celebrated likewise in the action of a sacramental meal. While care must be taken not to impose extrinsically a "theme" upon a given celebration—something that occurs all too often in our churches— one of the several ideas that are genuinely conveyed by the biblical readings of the day and the surrounding liturgical texts should be chosen and developed as the unifying message of the service.

11

This is so that the music, both congregational and choral, the readings and responses, the homily, the Prayer of the Faithful and the other texts (especially the opening prayer and the prayer after Communion) may all blend to form one clear proclamation of the Good News. Obviously I speak of an ideal that perhaps seldom will be fully realized. The role of music in the celebration, however, can be enormously helpful in achieving this goal, albeit imperfectly. A sensitive selection of hymns whose texts and melodies reinforce the central message of the day contributes mightily to the making of a good liturgical service. In fact there are time when the hymns and other musical portions of the service can actually "bail out" other parts of the celebration (e.g., the homily) that have failed to do their job.

I remember hearing, years ago, an Anglican priest (now a bishop in the Northwest) describe to a group of ministers and priests how he enlisted the aid of the choir in "getting the message across" at Sunday Eucharists. Early in the week he would select the theme of his homily from the biblical readings and the collect of the day. On Wednesday morning he would meet with the organist-choirmistress and together they would select congregational hymns and choral music that would reinforce the central theme he had chosen. That night he would come to the choir rehearsal and for about half an hour explain what he hoped to develop in his homily and how the music chosen reinforced his message. Invariably he would conclude by telling the members of the choir that although he well might fail to put across the message through preaching, he was confident that they would proclaim it adequately, indeed powerfully, through song. "Qui cantat bis orat." They who sing— and who encourage others to sing with robust faith—pray twice!

Again, while liturgy is not intended to effect initial faith-conversion, it can and does bolster flagging faith. Who among us comes to worship each Sunday with serene, unwavering, untroubled faith? Who among us does not doubt? Even if we have experienced genuine conversion to the Lord, we often find it hard to believe, to maintain a sense of vital contact with the unseen realities that are the objects of our faith. Here, again, music in the context of a community celebration can support and lift us up in our weakness. The singing of texts, especially those that challenge us by the depth of the mystery to which they point or by the awesomeness of what they demand, reminds us that our "statements" about God and our relationship with him are symbolic statements. This is not to relegate what we profess at worship to the level of "just poetry" or "mere rhetoric." But it is to be aware that all our language about ultimate reality, ultimate mystery, is incapable of bearing the depth of meaning to which our spoken human words so feebly point. The scholastics of old reminded us that in speaking of God and the things of God we are at best "homines balbutientes," poor stutterers. But just as those who stutter in speech can often sing with ease, so we who stutter in our words about faith can take courage and sing those words with a great measure of trust and belief. A friend of mine who for years struggled to hold on to his Christian faith once said, "I cannot say the creed but I can sing it."

Finally, we are told in article 2 that at liturgy we assemble to acknowledge God's love and "to stand in awe and praise." Once again music comes to our aid. All celebrations must be characterized by a primacy of thanksgiving and praise. "Let us give thanks to the Lord our God," an invitation to worship that comes to us from our Jewish forebears in the faith, introduces the Great Prayer of the Eucharist and expresses the mood or atmosphere that should envelop the entire act of worship. Hymns and choral music that evoke by word and melody a sense of wonder, praise and thanksgiving are appropriate at virtually any part of the liturgy. This is especially true at the entrance procession (we are a grateful people coming into the Lord's presence) and during and after the communion procession (with grateful hearts we taste and see the goodness of the Lord). The importance of reinforcing the central theme of the celebration does not mean that we are to look only for hymns that "say the same thing" as the biblical readings or the homily. Frequently we can effectively reinforce the message of the day by a hymn that gives voice in words of praise and thanksgiving to the sentiments of awe and gratitude that the more didactic portions of the liturgy inspire. If the message of the liturgy is always God's love for us (what else have we to proclaim and to celebrate?), then songs of praise should be ever in our hearts and on our lips. That has been the conviction of the Church from the time of Paul the Apostle to the present day. "Amantis est cantare'" it was said anciently; a lover cannot help bursting into song. Organists, instrumentalists, choirs, cantors—all who perform a ministry of music in our churches—please help us to do just that!

Coda. Two observations, by way of a postscript, concerning a possible revision of the text of articles 1 and 2. I have already suggested an expansion that would include an explicit treatment of the relation between liturgical celebrations and the faith community. I would add here that both for the two articles that formed the basis for my essay and for the other articles of "The Theology of Celebration" there is need of a slightly more developed text. The present form of this section as well as the rest of *Music in Catholic Worship* is first-rate. The introductory section, which lays the theological basis for the entire document, is so dense, however, that some of its richness and force might escape many a reader. I would estimate that two pages of text rather than simply one would suffice to open up more explicitly the theological wealth of this section.

Feel the Music

BY JOHN MELLOH

Fr. Melloh, Director of the Notre Dame Center for Pastoral Liturgy, also teaches liturgy for the Department of Theology and practices music.

Every liturgical document has two dimensions: a "better" and a "worse." Documents, on that account, need to be read quite critically; they should not be shunned like a pork vendor in downtown Jerusalem, nor should they be held in awe as though they had miraculously fallen from heaven, hermetically sealed in a Glad bag. Readers need to uncover the encased principles and ask perceptively how these principles find application in the pastoral situation. To do so is to be true to the best tradition of the Church and to further its growth. Progress is made only through analysis of such documents and their application to the liturgical celebration (Crichton, Ch. 1).

Music in Catholic Worship is a decade old. It has provided not only guidelines for the use of music in worship, but also sound theological principles. The first chapter offers a framework for approaching the liturgy and for coming to grips with the musical questions that have plagued Christians for centuries. First of all, it presumes that liturgy is an action, an outcome of responding to Jesus Christ in faith (Article 1). Second, this action is communitarian (Article 2). Third, the liturgical act is an affair of the heart (Article 4), involving not only the intellect and will (Article 3), but also the religious affections (Article 5). In short, the opening chapter describes, albeit in condensed phrases, the nature of the liturgical act and suggests summarily how Christians can actually be involved in the act itself. (Succeeding chapters explicate these principles with a view toward praxis.)

Having celebrated the rites revised by Vatican II and having put into practice the pastoral admonitions of *Music in Catholic Wor-*

ship, we need now to reflect on the current status of the liturgical act in general, and on music as an integral part of that act in particular. These reflections will provide a backdrop for closer scrutiny of the document and may allow us to refine both the guidelines and their applications. With this article I am offering my impressions of the *status questionis*—and they are really impressions, since they are not based on empirical data. They may be challenged, or, for that matter, roundly rejected—*Gratis asseritur, gratis negatur,* runs the old maxim— but they at least offer a point of departure. It seems to me that in the last ten years we have developed a renewed sense of community, a heightened sense of action, a deepened sense of authenticity and a more affective liturgy.

A renewed sense of community. The single most important contribution of Vatican II to the life of the Church is its reformed ecclesiology. The Church, a pilgrim people, is dynamic, not static. And the worship offered by the Church is offered by a social body; worship is an outcome of a community's living the conversion experience of dying and rising with Jesus.

It appears to me that the Church in the United States is grappling with this problem of *being* a community and expressing its life in worship. Liturgical celebrations are evolving—happily so. They are moving in the direction of genuinely shared activity. Witness, for example, the rooting of "new ministries" in the average parish: readers, eucharistic ministers, leaders of song. This points to the fact that we are overcoming the long-seated spectator approach to worship. The fact that ministries are shared among the community indicates growth and a return to traditional practice. With regard to music, specifically, we note that our congregations *are* singing. (I am not commenting on the quality of the music or its rendering.) And choirs, whose function in the past often was to provide a Muzak background to liturgy or to usurp truly congregational songs, have a different job description.

A heightened sense of action. The Church is discovering slowly and, we hope, surely the truism that liturgy is action. The worship event is engaging action, which not only expresses, but deepens the experience of *metanoia,* change of heart (Article 1). We are gradually overcoming a resistance to ritual acts born of the experience with all too often meaningless formalistic rituals.

The questions we are asking have changed. Perceptive liturgical committees are inquiring: How can this posture, this procession, this gesture of this dance be religious acts for us? Less central questions—important immediately after the revision of the rites— are giving way to raising the deeper issues that are of ultimate concern.

A deepened sense of authenticity. Article 3 comments on genuineness and asserts boldly (though perhaps in a somewhat unrefined manner) that "we are celebrating... when everything we do is . . . authentic." In the wake of Vatican II, the United States saw the growth of "experimental" liturgies; one of the main purposes of these events seemed to be to make liturgy relevant (to whom? by what standards?) and meaningful (for whom? at what price?) (Crichton, pp. 39 ff). Perhaps the innovators (or instigators) were trying to *make* "everything" relevant. The days of uncontrolled (and somewhat mindless) celebrations have passed. But the underlying question—the one that spawned the growth of such underground church groups—is with us: Is our worship meaningful? Is it authentic?

A linear approach, somewhat wooden, was taken by many experimenters. *Change* (or even mutilate) the liturgical act so that *it* becomes relevant. The other possible approach to the answer was neglected: How must we, as a community, change—along with the rite—so that we can enter meaningfully into it? The emphasis on the RCIA document and serious concern about initiatory praxis, for example, indicates that there is hope for the alternative approach to the question.

A more affective liturgy. "Lift up your hearts." This introduction to the Eucharistic Prayer could well be the initial invitation to worship. Liturgy is an affair of the heart. *Music in Catholic Worship* rightly contextualizes the acts of worship as "signs of love" (Article 4). Liturgy is nothing more and nothing less than a love affair between God and the assembly.

In an age when liturgical law reigned supreme (at least notionally), the "objective" character of worship was first and foremost. "Subjectivity" was suspect; attendant affections were to be scrutinized scrupulously, because intellect and will governed the heart.

In the United States, an "Anglo-Saxon" approach has often been taken vis-a-vis the place (or lack of it) of emotions in worship. The mere thought of religious enthusiasm or the sight of a revival tent was enough to bring scorn to the lips of many practicing Roman Catholics. Rightly afraid of rampant emotionalism, the Roman worshipers may have effectively ceded the place of genuine emotions in worship.

True worship is not only cerebral, but emotive (Micks, Chapter 3). Praying liturgically is an act of the whole person, mind and heart (or however you wish to phrase it). The duality of matter and spirit, body and soul, is still operative in our attitudes toward worship and needs further scrutiny.

Having given my brief analysis of the current situation, I would like to focus specifically on the contributions of Articles 3, 4 and 5 of *Music in Catholic Worship* to a revitalized sense of worship. The above commentary should provide a basis for some comments specifically related to liturgy as a musical event.

A renewed sense of community. "We are celebrating when we

involve ourselves meaningfully in the thoughts, words, songs and gestures of the worshiping community" (Article 3). Worship, ecclesial prayer offered in assembly, is involvement—in the songs, gestures, thoughts and words of the action. This involvement, however, flows from the lifestyle of the believers. It is because they are involved in the life of Jesus and because they are involved in the building up of the social Body of Christ that they can be involved in the act of worship.

Singing with one voice can bolster a sense of community, but only if such a sense is already extant. Singing together does not create community ex nihilo. Real and strong feelings of belonging can be produced through involvement in common song and may speak to the mystery of fellowship in the Church. Diversity and individuality are put into perspective through common song (and common action, for that matter); we function as a unit when we sing God's praises together (Gelineau, p. 441).

Does our music do all that? Really? Is koinonia fostered by song? If music is to do that, then both text and melody must be inherently capable of welding the assembly together. One of the reasons, I believe, why we cringe at some 19th-century hymns is that their texts are excessively individualistic (to say nothing of the overly sentimental affections expressed). Text needs to challenge the assembly—theologically. If we want to "mean the words" (Article 3), then we need texts that express mainline Catholic tradition in appropriate 20th-century language (cf. Crichton, Ch. 3–4).

Moreover, if the melody is to serve as "congregational glue," it had better be strong and vigorous. Uninteresting melody lines—trite tunes—can never live up to that expectation.

A heightened sense of action. One of the functions of music in worship is to accompany ritual action. If we want "to do what is done" (Article 3), then the music truly must be ministerial. It needs to provide a "minimal catechetical explanation"—in a richly ambiguous and poetic manner—of the ritual action, providing an insight into the communal activity of the assembly.

Are we still singing music not integral to the essential actions of the liturgy? Do echoes of old Marian favorites still persist as unrelated "accompaniment" to the preparation of table and gifts? And if such refrains are used, do we sense their inadequacy? Is the Communion rite at a celebration of Eucharist on the Fourth of July, for example, blemished by a rousing rendition of "America, the Beautiful"?

To allow music to be integral to worship calls for sound judgment on the part of liturgical planners. Congruence and consistency between action and musical word is demanded.

A sense of authenticity. Ritual action can be cathartic—it can relieve tension and move participants to an inchoative ecstasy. But this is not the primary purpose of ritual action. Repeated patterns of social behavior invested with religious significance—rites, in a word—do give "bodily expression to faith as we celebrate" (Article 5). In doing so, the rite forms the believers. Rite, a *habitus* in the scholastic sense of the word, forms attitudes (Langer, *Philosophy in a New Key*).

Ritual action is evocative and expressive; it summons and projects ways of understanding our world (Micks, Ch. 3). But the rite is not always effective; sometimes it doesn't work. The rite will have a chance at being effective only if the believer can enter freely into the act, whether it be ritual dance, ritual song or ritual movement. The community needs to rediscover "a whole world of acts which have become atrophied" (Guardini, p. 24); only through entering the act can we "mean" what we do.

Giving oneself over to the rite creates attitudes. Assuming a posture of reverence gives us a chance to *be* reverent; joyfully singing praise allows us to *be* thankful; listening attentively moves us to *be* meditative. Our initial dispositions are thus deepened and furthered.

Such an ideal is possible only if we submit (not slavishly, but humanly) to the power of rite and symbol. Banal musical compositions, ersatz art, stereotyped stiff gestures will never provide an ethos that encourages entering personally into the assembly's actions.

An affective liturgy. "I wept at the beauty of your hymns and canticles, and was powerfully moved at the sweet sound of your Church singing. These sounds flowed into my ears and truth streamed into my heart." (Augustine, *Confessions*, IX, 397). Faith can be stimulated by our music—when it is inspiring, when it is a symbolic utterance replete with Christian meaning (not only in text, but in the expression). Augustine was taken by the beauty of the musical art and his faith strengthened. There was a connection between the emotional impact of song and truth that resided in the heart.

Our musical art is the "creation of forms symbolic of human feeling." "The performing congregation's attitudes and religious feelings are formed and shaped under the aegis of music; the import of music is the pattern of feeling the pattern of life itself as it is felt and directly known" (Langer, p. 40). For those who hear with Christian ears and sing with Christian lips, this outpouring of life in musical form is nothing but the expression in sound of the one mystery, that of Jesus' dying and rising. Beethoven is reported to have said: "What is to reach the heart must come from above, if it does not come then, it will be nothing but notes—body without spirit."

Through singing hymns and canticles, through listening to instrumental music—through being moved by musical artistry—the Christian appropriates the great *mysterium*. The mystery touches our hearts; our feelings are formed; our bodies, already enspirited, are even more vivified.

"We rise above our own feelings to respond to God in prayer" (Article 5). I believe that such phraseology is misleading. Christians, in the very act of celebrating, are forming attitudes of faith, forming religious affections. The assembly does not rise above its feelings, but rather, in entering freely into the ritual act, allows the feelings to be transformed, to be touched and shaped by the presence of the transcendent and immanent Godhead.

If there are acts of the will involved in liturgical celebration—and there are—they are not for the dismissal or control of the feeling states, but are, on the contrary, directed toward choosing to give oneself over to the communal action of the assembly. "In the liturgy we act in order to be acted upon" (Grimes, p. 134). In our positing of the liturgical integrated act of the community, we make ourselves the very symbols that speak—mind and heart, body and spirit, flesh and bone, emotion and will (cf. Matthews and Berntsen).

Roman Guardini in 1964 struck the chord: "The question is . . . whether we shall relearn a forgotten way of doing things and recapture lost attitudes" (Guardini, p. 24). We are in the process of relearning and recapturing. The questions we have are better questions, even if we still do not have better answers. Progress is being made. We are a pilgrim people in via, ever in via.

Our liturgical celebrations, enriched by the sound principles in Music in Catholic Worship, give testimony to a renewed sense of community, but the question is still with us: Is there a sufficient communitarian foundation to support a worship in koinonia, genuine Christian fellowship? Our sense of liturgy as action is heightened, but we still query: Is our integrated liturgical act musical in its very structure? A deepening sense of authenticity is permeating the Church at celebration, while we pose the question: How must we change in order to allow the power of rite to be effective in our lives? Worship that is all too cerebral is giving way to a more affective liturgy, and we ask: Can we offer really heartfelt praise?

REFERENCES

Berntsen, John A. "Christian Affections and the Catechumenate." Worship 52 (1978), 194–211.

Crichton, J. D. The Once and Future Liturgy, Paulist Press, 1977.

Gelineau, Josef, S.J. "Music and Singing in the Liturgy," in: The Study of Liturgy, Ed. Cheslyn Jones, et al. Oxford University Press, 1978.

Grimes, Ronald L. "Modes of Ritual Necessity." Worship 53 (1979), 126–34.

Guardini, Romano. "A Letter from Romano Guardini." *Herder Correspondence,* Special Issue, 1964, 24–28.

Langer, Susanne. *Feeling and Warmth.* Scribners, 1953.

Matthews, Gareth B. "Bodily Motions and Religious Feelings." *Canadian Journal of Philosophy* 1 (1971), 75–87.

Micks, Marianne. *The Future Present.* Seabury Press, 1970.

COMMENTARY ON 6–7

Keep It the Way It Is!

BY EUGENE WALSH

Fr. Walsh publishes lectures and gives workshops on the theory and practice of effective sacramental celebration.

"Good celebrations foster and nourish faith. Poor celebrations weaken and destroy faith." These sentences have become the all-time favorite quotation from the document we are writing about. They have become a kind of touchstone of what is new and different in the understanding of the sacramental theology of our time. They say very simply that sacramental signs give life or deprive life according to the manner in which they are done.

This quotable quote belongs to Sections 6 and 7 of the document. Sections 6 and 7 in turn belong as an organic part of the entire first section, numbers 1–9. And this entire first section stands as a simple, almost classic expression of the theology of sacrament and celebration we are expected to bring to life today.

I thought initially that the document *Music in Catholic Worship* should be revised and rewritten. Now I want to suggest that the document not be revised or rewritten. Keep it the way it is. It is a forthright document that says well what needs to be said. It is a good summary and a good outline, which is what it was meant to be. Any rewriting would necessarily expand it into a sizable book. And that is definitely what we do not need.

I suggest, therefore, that the document be edited for sexist language and for format, perhaps that it be expanded carefully to address what needs to be said about other sacraments.[1]

What needs to be done beyond simple reediting is to spell out in much more detail and in simple language for music ministers (for all who celebrate) the sacramental theology that is summarized in the first nine articles of the document. We are at such a point in renewal that we cannot make a life-giving celebration of Sunday Mass unless we work out the principles of the "new" theology in a form that can be communicated to everyone. Everyone who gathers on Sunday to celebrate Eucharist must know *why* they are doing what they are doing. If they do not, they simply cannot make the life-giving signs that make a good celebration. They cannot do it well. "Faith grows when it is *well* expressed in celebration." Failure to understand the "new" sacramental theology is, I think, the biggest reason why so many Sunday Mass celebrations are so boring and not life-giving.

More specifically there is need to spell out for music composers and music planners and music makers what it means to make musical signs that are "humanly attractive" and signs that are "clear and compelling."

The task in front of us at this moment in history is not to revise a document that stands already as a fine summary of principles. The task is to provide materials that spell out the implications already contained in the document. There are a number of ways to do this. One is to publicize existing materials that already do the spelling out. My own published materials are exactly and specifically such an attempt. They have been received as such, recognized as such, and are working. (He said modestly.) Another is to put out an accompanying study text to this present document such as has been done for the different sacramental rites. However it is done, the immediate task is not more theory. It is to spell out what the theory means and how to make it work in practice.

The materials contained in Sections VI and VII raise three issues that need to be spelled out: the issue of sacraments as life-giving signs; the issue of sacraments as attractive human communication; and the issue of sacraments as clear and compelling signs.

First, the idea of sacraments as life-giving signs means very simply that sacraments *are* signs. The whole sacrament is the whole sign, and the whole sign is the whole sacrament. You cannot split sacraments into outer form and inner reality any more than you can split a human person into outer form and inner reality. You can distinguish but you cannot separate. When you take away the outer form—the sign that the person is and through which the person expresses self—you kill the person. The same is true for a sacrament.

Sacraments, therefore, are signs of human communication and are subject to all the laws of human communication. This means that sacraments are life-giving only when life-giving people make life-giving signs. They are life-depriving when they are empty or routine or perfunctory. As the sign flourishes, so the sacrament flourishes. As the sign fails, so the sacrament fails.

All this and much more of the same needs to be spelled out as clearly as possible in any study text that would accompany the document. All who celebrate have got to understand this sacramental theology or they are doomed to make poor signs, and poor signs make poor celebrations and . . . there we go again.

This personal investment is not a "gut-spilling" event for the person who invests. It has a clear object and purpose. It has a clear discipline. Personal investment is for the purpose of engaging and supporting others is the common act of worship. Any personal investment that is not captured by this discipline becomes an ego trip and an affront to the celebrating community.

Second, the idea of sacraments as attractive human communication means that the life-giving signs must be fitting and acceptable to the people who make them and to the people for whom they are made. Another way of putting it is to say that sacramental signs become more and more humanly attractive as they are subject to the discipline of the principles of all art: unity, harmony, emphasis. There is a difference between "huggy-kissy-bear" and warm disciplined human communication. Ritual is precisely the business of disciplining human communication so that it is strong and beautiful and loving for all the different kinds of people that celebrate. Ministers of worship are not expected to achieve high art in this area. They are expected, however, to achieve the discipline of the skill, because they are capable of gaining the skill. All this and much more needs to be spelled out in detail for the music minister.

Third, the idea of sacraments as "clear and compelling" signs means that signs of sacramental celebration must communicate "clearly and compellingly" what is there to be communicated. The Eucharist, for instance, is a definite reality that has its own structure and dynamic. The musical signs we make must serve to reveal that structure so that it shines clear for all to behold. Enlightened music ministers use their musical signs very carefully to reveal the beauty that "lies deep down in things."

There is no excuse to program music for Sunday Mass in an undisciplined and careless way, in a way that suits the personal taste of people who really do not know what they are doing. We have now a clear picture of the pattern and the dynamic of a Eucharistic celebration. We know the important parts of the Mass and the less important parts. We know that we can no longer follow patterns inherited from the recent past: the "high Mass" pattern, the "four hymn" syndrome. These no longer work. They render the Eucharistic sign confused and ambiguous. The sign becomes less revealing, therefore less life-giving. Nostalgia is not a good enough reason to hold onto anything of the past when it clearly does not fit, when it clearly gets in the way. Once you bring out clearly the pattern and structure of the Eucharistic action and its dynamic, there are many other creative ways to use the best of our inherited tradition.

People who know what they are doing will look first to make the two major events of the Eucharistic action shine with as much brilliance as possible—the Liturgy of the Word and the Liturgy of the Eucharist. To enhance the Word they will look for a beautiful and carefully crafted responsorial psalm and for a strong gospel acclamation. They will see that these are carefully integrated with the other elements of the Liturgy of the Word: reading, listening, silence. They will be assured that these choices will be executed in a manner that will enhance the power and strength of this action. They will carefully design the structure and the dynamic flow.

Music ministers who know their stuff will give the same attention to the Eucharistic Prayer. They will seek out strong, vigorous acclamations and see that the community learns them by heart. They will make sure that these "shouts" of praise and blessing and remembrance are truly shouts and not weak and ineffectual whimpers. They will find musical and artistic ways to link the acclamation with its particular invitation so that the acclamation springs spontaneously and immediately from its invitation without benefit of foolish and delaying introductions.

For the same reason enlightened and competent music ministers will take care not to clutter up the Entrance Rite. They know that one good, strong opening hymn is called for and that is enough. They will be reluctant to sing "Lord Have Mercy" and "Glory to God" because this defeats the purpose of the Entrance Rite and gives out confusing signals. Will the real part of this Eucharistic celebration please stand up? They will give the same attention to reduce the musical signs of the Preparation of Gifts. No song for the people most of the time; let them relax; just fine instrumental music or a choral offering. If the people must sing—please, no songs about bread and wine.

[1]Editor's note: this sentence refers to the 1972 edition of *Music In Catholic Worship*, and was written before the revised edition of MCW or the publication of *Liturgical Music Today*.

Mean What You Sign

BY THOMAS A. KROSNICKI

Fr. Krosnicki is the Executive Director for the Bishops' Committee on the Liturgy, the National Conference of Catholic Bishops.

Section I of *Music in Catholic Worship* concludes with two articles addressing the question of signs in liturgical celebrations (Articles 8–9). In fact, these articles reiterate and briefly expand an earlier statement of the document: ". . . signs are vehicles of communication and instruments of faith, they must be simple and comprehensible" (Article 7).

Without doubt the articles under consideration from the 1972 music document remain valid statements of basic liturgical principles. The distinction generally made between signs and symbols, alluded to in Articles 5–7, is maintained. Sign, however, is understood in the broadest context. Whatever is intended to make a statement in the liturgical celebration is in effect a sign. Sign is comprehensive: the gathering, gestures, art, architecture, language (spoken and sung), and so on. Thus, these introductory articles are as applicable to the sign of the assembly as to the celebrant's gestures over the gifts placed upon the altar.

Three principles emerge from Articles 8 and 9 of this document: 1. Signs should be clear and unencumbered; 2. Signs should not be repeated unnecessarily; 3. Signs as a part of the faith experience of the celebrants should need no explanation. A brief consideration of each of these principles in the light of our recent experience will assist in the evaluation of these two articles from the well-studied 1972 music document.

Signs should be clear and unencumbered. As with any type of statement, clarity is essential for signs to be comprehended and effective. Needless meandering blocks communication; a sentence really needs only a subject and predicate!

The Vatican II revision of liturgical rites did much to clarify and disentangle the signs of celebrations from centuries of unnecessary accretions. Consideration was given to both the clarification of the purpose of the sign (what it is to say and do) as well as its proper execution (how it is to be said and done). The reform in this regard is generally judged positively.

This is not to say that the basic Roman reform is definitive, since any statement is made in the context of a particular time and culture. Thus, it is not difficult to understand that we recognize elements in the present Eucharistic ritual where the principle of clarity needs to be reapplied. One thinks, for example, of the washing of hands and the private prayers of the celebrant during the Presentation of the Gifts. Another example is the Sign of Peace. Could it be that in the American cultural experience this sign can signify only one thing, a greeting of welcome? If this is true, then it is imperative that the present position of this sign be reconsidered. Many see these three signs as ambiguous liturgical statements.

The three-study of the structural element of the *Ordo Missae,* recently decided upon by the Bishops' Committee on the Liturgy, is an example of ongoing concern for the quality of each liturgical statement and ultimately of the quality of the entire prayer statement of the community as such.

Such consideration must also be given to the type of statement music makes within the liturgical action. It betrays, for example, one's understanding of community participation and how well one has comprehended the function of the musical signs within the various parts of the given celebration.

Notice that the 1972 document states that signs should be *short* in addition to being clear and unencumbered. I would suggest omitting "short" from the paragraph in any future revision of the text since brevity is not always a criterion of effective signs if, by sign, one accepts the comprehensive understanding of liturgical sign statement.

Signs should not be repeated unnecessarily. Those of us who recall celebrating the Eucharist prior to the revisions of 1969 recognize the wisdom of this principle. The numerous signs of the cross previously made over the gifts were redundant to say the least! Whereas structural repetition has been attended to in the revision of the liturgical rites, there are areas where more attention is called for.

In art and architecture the application of this second principle is just getting under way. The multiplication of altars, images of saints, and so on, within the one liturgical space is now recognized as redundant (see: *Environment and Art in Catholic Worship,* no. 72). In music this principle is valid in most instances. Yet, recently I participated in a Eucharistic celebration where, after Communion, a choir sang a selection that virtually repeated the institution narrative of the Eucharistic Prayer. A fine piece of music, yes; an example of unnecessary and inappropriate repetition, nevertheless.

The operative word in this principle seems to be "unnecessary." Repetition in musical sign statements, for example, is effective as experienced in the present Penitential Rite and the refrain of the Responsorial Psalm. Even the "Lamb of God" may be properly extended to be functionally repetitious, as it accompanies the breaking of the bread.

Signs as a part of the faith experience of the celebrants should need no explanation. Of the three suggested principles, this is the most difficult. First of all, I would suggest that the principle be qualified in such a way as to state clearly that no explanation of the sign statements is needed *with the initiated.* In other words, the signs might at times be comprehensible only to those of the community of faith and are not necessarily comprehensible to those outside of it. The reasons for this are simple. We are working with various levels of understanding of interpretation of the sign statements. Thus, on the first level of understanding it is clear to all that the sign of bread and wine is simply that—a sign of foodstuff. Yet, the sign statement says something quite beyond the obvious when understood on a deeper level of faith interpretation. Thus, to the initiated the bread and wine signs within the Eucharist are eventually read as body and blood. It is the faith of the initiated that enables them to read the signs correctly by interlacing such elements as Christian understanding, memory and imagination.

This process is not always easy, since the faith-sign-statement goes beyond the purely empirical order, reaching into the non-cognitive. Americans, with an obsession for the "real," find it difficult to enter into the deeper orders of sign reality. Is that why we are more comfortable with metaphors than symbols? Could it also be that many of the signs presently designed are ill-equipped to assist the individual and community to go beyond the first level of meaning? How aesthetic are the signs we use in the areas of environment, art and music? On the one hand, we too often find what is decidedly in poor taste, if not outright vulgar, presented to the community. It is then that the environment of worship is bound to become the locus of conflict. On the other hand, what response is given to those places where the liturgical statement or signs employed are evocative, expressive and effective? Then they have truly become tools of good communication.

The three principles outlined in Articles 8 and 9 remain valid. A sign as a statement is both informative and evocative. Yet, to truly savor a "Hot Meals" sign, it helps to be a *hungry* traveler.

Music in Catholic Worship: Section II

PASTORAL PLANNING FOR CELEBRATION

PASTORAL PLANNING FOR CELEBRATION

10. The responsibility for effective pastoral celebration in a parish community falls upon all those who exercise major roles in the liturgy. "The particular preparation for each liturgical celebration should be done in a spirit of cooperation by all parties concerned, under the guidance of the rector of the church, whether it be ritual, pastoral, or musical matters."[2] In practice this ordinarily means an organized "planning team" or committee which meets regularly to achieve creative and coordinated worship and a good use of the liturgical and musical options of a flexible liturgy.

11. The power of a liturgical celebration to share faith will frequently depend upon its unity—a unity drawn from the liturgical feast or season or from the readings appointed in the lectionary as well as artistic unity flowing from the skillful and sensitive selection of options, music, and related arts. The sacred scriptures ought to be the source and inspiration of sound planning for it is of the very nature of celebration that people hear the saving words and works of the Lord and then respond in meaningful signs and symbols. Where the readings of the lectionary possess a thematic unity, the other elements ought to be so arranged as to constitute a setting for and response to the message of the Word.

12. The planning team or committee is headed by the priest (celebrant and homilist) for no congregation can experience the security of a unified celebration if that unity is not grasped by the one who presides, as well as by those who have special roles. The planning group should include those with the knowledge and artistic skills needed in celebration:

men and women trained in music, poetry, and art, and familiar with current resources in these areas; men and women sensitive also to the presentday thirst of so many riches of scripture, theology, and prayer. It is always good to include some members of the congregation who have not taken special roles in the celebrations so that honest evaluations can be made.

13. The planning should go beyond the choosing of options, songs, and ministers to the composition of such texts as the brief introduction, general intercessions, and other appropriate comments as provided in the *General Instruction of the Roman Missal.* How people are invited to join in a particular song may be as important as the choice of the song itself.

14. In planning pastoral celebrations the congregation, the occasion, and the celebrant must be taken into consideration.

The Congregation

15. "The pastoral effectiveness of a celebration will be heightened if the texts of readings, prayers, and songs correspond as closely as possible to the needs, religious disposition and aptitude of the participants."[3] A type of celebration suitable for a youth group may not fit in a retirement home; a more formal style effective in a parish church may be inappropriate in a home liturgy. The music used should be within the competence of most of the worshippers. It should suit their age-level, cultural background, and level of faith.

16. Variations in level of faith raise special problems. Liturgical celebration presupposes a minimum of biblical knowledge and a deep commitment of living faith. If these are lacking, there might arise the tendency to use the liturgy as a tool of evangelization. Greater liberty in the choice of music and style of celebration may be required as the participants are led toward that day when they can share their growing faith as members of the Christian community. Songs like the psalms may create rather than solve problems where faith is weak. Music, chosen with care, can serve as a bridge to faith as well as an expression of it.

17. The diversity of people present at a parish liturgy gives rise to a further problem. Can the same parish liturgy be an authentic expression for a grade school girl, her college-age brother, their married sister with her young family, their parents and grandparents? Can it satisfy the theologically and musically educated along with those lacking in training? Can it please those who seek a more informal style of celebration? The planning team must consider the general makeup of the total community. Each Christian must keep in mind that to live and worship in community often demands a personal sacrifice. All must be willing to share likes and dislikes with those whose ideas and experience may be quite unlike their own.

18. Often the problem of diversity can be mitigated by supplementing the parish Sunday celebration with special celebrations for smaller homogeneous groups. "The need of the faithful of a particular cultural background or of a particular age level may often be met by a music that can serve as a congenial, liturgically oriented expression of prayer."[4] The music and other options may then be more easily suited to the particular group celebrating. Celebration in such groups, "in which the genuine sense of community is more readily experienced, can contribute significantly to growth in awareness of the parish as community, especially when all the faithful participate in the parish Mass on the Lord's day."[5] Nevertheless, it would be out of harmony with the Lord's wish for unity in his Church if believers were to worship only in such homogeneous groupings.[6]

The Occasion

19. The same congregation will want to celebrate in a variety of ways. During the course of the year the different mysteries of redemption are celebrated in the Mass so that in some way they are made present.[7] Each feast and season has its own spirit and its own music. The penitential occasions demand more restraint. The great feasts demand more solemnity. Solemnity, however, depends less on the ornateness of song and magnificence of ceremonial than on worthy and religious celebration.[8]

20. Generally a congregation or choir will want to sing more on the great feasts like Christmas and Easter and less in the season through the year. Important events in family and parish life will suggest fuller programs of song. Sundays will be celebrated with variety but always as befits the day of the Lord. All liturgies, from the very simple to the most ornate, must be truly pastoral and prayerful.

The Celebrant

21. No other single factor affects the liturgy as much as the attitude, style, and bearing of the celebrant: his sincere faith and warmth as he welcomes the worshipping community; his human naturalness combined with dignity and seriousness as he breaks the Bread of Word and Eucharist.

22. The style and pattern of song ought to facilitate the effectiveness of a good celebrant. His role is enhanced when he is capable of rendering some of his parts in song and he should be encouraged to do so. What he cannot sing well and effectively he ought to recite. If capable of singing, he ought, for the sake of people, to rehearse carefully the sung parts that would contribute to their celebration.[9]

First, You Must Plan. . .

BY JOHN FOLEY

Rev. John Foley, SJ is a composer and member of the St. Louis Jesuits.

In former days, the Mass was "always the same" from day to day, from land to land. Certain elements changed regularly, but these were carefully defined and not open to "creative intervention." Priests and musicians knew what to be ready for each Sunday. This is no longer so. Even though much is still prescribed, and essential experimentation is discouraged, the new liturgy now must be creatively reviewed each week, on pain of confusion or failure. "Flexibility reigns supreme," states *Music in Catholic Worship*. Within the legislated format, "a sense of artistry and a deep knowledge of the rhythm of the liturgical action" are necessary in order to "combine the many options into an effective whole" (*MCW* #76).

The unity of the Eucharistic liturgy is offered to us in germ form only. It is no longer possible to just "say a Mass," without forethought and prayer, if that Mass is to hang together, if it is to "foster and nourish faith." Whether this state of affairs is realistic or even possible on a large scale is a topic for later debate; the fact is that even for the lone priest at the seven a.m. Mass, unified worship must be worked at and chosen, or it will not happen at all.

"The sacred scriptures ought to be the source and inspiration of sound planning for it is the very nature of celebration that people *hear the saving words and works of the Lord and then respond in meaningful signs and symbols*" (emphasis mine; *MCW* #11). Luke's gospel says the same thing: "Blest are those who hear the word of God and keep it." Doing follows hearing. All the actions of the Mass are to be expressions of and responses to the Lord as proclaimed that day, that season.

In practice, then, liturgy requires its ministers to have absorbed the unity present in the readings of the day. Before the planning, and certainly before the liturgy happens, they must find a way to sense (intuit, contemplate, hear, "understand," feel) the Word of God with the nuances of the particular day. Ordinarily this means a period or more of prayerful listening, either privately or within a team meeting.

In fact, the team meeting can be the perfect place for a contemplative reading of the Scripture (aloud) and a brief, prayerful sharing of how the Word touches the individuals in the group. Normally statements of moods and feelings are more helpful than theoretical explanations. For example, the statement "I felt elated when I heard the words 'Come to me, all who are burdened'. . . ." aids the process more than "Christ is telling us that we should come to him when we are needy, not seek out the things of this world." This latter, while not wrong, is too much a completed homiletic statement; articulation of an insight or of a theme is not necessary at this point. True unity emerges less from a "theme" than from the touch of the Lord's words in our hearts.

Once we begin to grasp the message in the context of the liturgical feast or season, it can be the guide and content of the liturgical options of the day. Which preface is used, and is it sung? Which Eucharistic Prayer is chosen? Is the acclamation to be sung or spoken, and what mood does either create? As many as 50 musical choices stand open to be made in medium- and large-scale liturgies. The effect will be haphazard or worse unless the people making the choices have thought through and felt the reasons beforehand. Too many congregations see a bewildering series of rubrical events when they go to Sunday Mass, a jumble of words and gestures for which they can discover only the most basic rationale: "That's the way it's done now." But if the choices proceed from a unified whole and are made to serve the whole, effective liturgy blossoms forth.

Who is to be responsible for all this hearing and choosing? In small liturgies of certain types, it may possibly be the priest alone. If it is, the responsibility falls to him to contemplate the Word of Scripture ahead of time and let that Word pervade the assembly. But more likely, in Sunday liturgies for instance, the roles diversify, because the paticipating assembly is larger. The ministers of the Mass—the priest, the deacon, the readers, the musician(s) (cantor, choir director, folk leader, or organist) and a representative of the congregation—therefore must meet and draw their particular area of responsibility into the framework of the whole.

"In practice," says *MCW*, "this ordinarily means an organized 'planning team' or committee which meets regularly to achieve creative and coordinated worship and a good use of the liturgical and musical options of a flexible liturgy" (*MCW* #10). There are problems, many problems, with the "planning team" concept, as anyone knows who has sat on one. But it is an attempt to broaden the responsibility for the liturgy in a unified manner. If parish liturgists can listen to Scripture and draw unity from it in some other way, so be it. But a planning team is the basic approach and can work well if the right people are on it, and if all other things are equal.

Of course, they never are, and so it is important not to enshrine the planning team approach. Many modifications may have to be made according to the personalities and abilities of the people involved. Some choir directors may find the requirement of one or more drawn-out planning session per week more than they can manage. Maybe such individuals could send a representative to the meetings or meet informally with another minister of the Mass to find out what happened at the session. Sometimes, given time limitations and varying temperaments, it might be better to skip the meeting idea altogether and simply confer informally. Each team has to work out its own best way of sensing the unity and helping it come to be.

Experience shows that the priest does not necessarily have to be the head of the team. As homilist and presider over the liturgy he naturally has more effect on the tone of the Mass than others. If his homily, for instance, is at odds with the general feel of the music, or if he does not grasp the tone of the readings, one of the central unifying elements in the Mass will be lost. But none of this need elect him head of the planning team. He may be a poor group leader. Worry about the formality of a meeting might distract him from his own preparation for Mass. Not everyone can listen and plan and lead all at the same time.

If there is another team member who can serve as leader from meeting to meeting, the priest might better be at the meeting as a participating member, collecting data, seeing how the readings affect the others, sharing in the planning. He then goes away to use the data as material for further prayer and reflection.

MCW gives an extraordinarily optimistic checklist for possible committee members. The planning team "should include those with the knowledge and artistic skills needed in celebration: men and women trained in music, poetry, and art, and knowledge in current resources in these areas; men and women sensitive also to the present day thirst of so many [for the] riches of scripture, theology, and prayer" (*MCW* #12). This is a tall order indeed. Add to the list that they must be willing! Obviously, such people are hard to find. Many parishes would be grateful just to locate a good choirleader or cantor, much less a group of people with all these skills.

Yet, given the need to unify each large-scale Mass (as opposed to merely "saying" it), such a list of talents is perhaps good as an ideal to shoot for. The planning committee must be more than a simple democratic selection of parish members if the liturgy is to be effective. Nor can it be just a collection of the most willing bodies in the parish. The document is correct in reminding us that specific skills and sensitivities are required for the various roles in the liturgy. The closer we can get to the ideal, the better.

Practially speaking, the pastor might start out looking for just one individual who tends toward the qualifications listed. A person somewhat willing, skilled in leadership, and knowledgeable about things liturgical, would make a fine leader of the planning sessions. S/he could shepherd the others, making best use of their talents and insights in the meeting, and above all, keep the meeting going. Experience shows that one such individual can mean the difference between topnotch meetings and long, drawn out, barely effective ones. As other such members are found, they can be added to the roster.

However optimistic the list of qualifications in MCW may be, there is still one glaring and serious omission: skill in group communication and cooperation. If it is true that liturgical ministers must absorb and plan a Eucharist ahead of time, and if, because of that, team meetings are necessary in the Catholic Church, then we Catholics must acquire the skills necessary to have good meetings. Anyone who has been frightened of speaking out in a group, or frustrated by long meetings with little results, or angered by individuals who can talk a meeting into the ground, will know instantly that good meetings require able participants, and that these are rare indeed.

A pastor who is really interested in his planners, for instance, might want to raise money for their participation in a good communications workshop. These sessions, run by experts, can last three days or two weeks, depending on what is desired, and can add a joy and efficiency to meetings that will overcome many other defects. At the very least, the pastor should salt any planning team with members who have the specific ability to work with others in a meeting.

Finally, a team must severely limit the number of things it tries to do. A committee may possibly be able to appoint someone to compose a "brief introduction, general intercessions, and other appropriate comments" (MCW #14), but it will certainly not be able to do such composition itself. As the saying goes, if a committee wrote it, no one wrote it. A team can make sure these items are being done well without having to write them itself. An evaluation session on last week's liturgy, if it were strictly limited as to length, would be a more efficient manner of handling the matter.

Because the members of a planning team are necessarily people who have full-time jobs elsewhere, plus family obligations, they will not ordinarily be pleading for more and longer meetings. A strict time limit on all meetings will help a good number of people take part. Because of this, it is probably never possible for a committee to do a good job in the "choosing of options, songs, and ministers" for a liturgy (*MCW* #13). Good choices take time and specialized ability; the minister of the area in question would most likely make them best, especially if s/he and the others had prayerfully heard and focused the readings. The music selections are a particularly good example of this. Occasionally the music minister may want help choosing the music, but usually s/he should use his or her ability without interference from the committee. The context is enough to ensure unity. Of course, the musician should later seek reactions to the music s/he used at the liturgy.

We can argue about how difficult or unrealistic it is for the Church to leave so many options open each Sunday, to make the Mass so flexible that its very unity is dependent on individuals. The format does seem to ask too much of us on a regular basis, more than is ordinarily possible. It does tend to fall apart when artistic, trained, knowledgeable teams are not at work (and are they not the exception rather than the rule?). Nevertheless, whatever we may think, the one-man-rule of the priest is over now, and the participation of the congregation through various roles and through teamwork is upon us. Let us bend all efforts and send up all prayer to make it work.

Congregations Differ— So Plan for It

BY RALPH KEIFER

Dr. Keifer is a Professor of Liturgy at Catholic Theological Union, Chicago, Illinois.

It is gratifying to observe that just a few years after the publication of *Music in Catholic Worship*, most of its concerns have become common coin among those with an interest in parish worship. For all the lip service we may give to some of the principles articulated in the section on "The Congregation" (Nos. 15–18), when we come to actual practice, at least we have become sensitized to the worship needs of various groupings. What we are doing about it all is another question. One of the reasons we are still at loose ends on many of the issues raised in this section is not inattention to its principles. Rather, it is because we all share its (now) evident weaknesses. We have, in a word, grown into its presuppositions without growing beyond them in such a way that we could achieve its (still worthwhile) goals.

The weaknesses of this section are that on one hand it is too timid, and on the other, it poses some thorny questions inadequately. If we are to deal constructively with this section of *Music in Catholic Worship*, we have to distinguish between its praiseworthy aim (unity in diversity, respecting the needs of real people) and its somewhat timid and one-sided formulation of the issue. If we are to achieve a worship pattern that does celebrate our unity in diversity, we will need both courage and a sharpening of perception.

The Sacramentary reminds us that it is not simply a matter of choosing appropriate music, but also that there is a need to have readings, prayers and songs coherently interrelated. Yet even the very limited and restricted *Directory for Masses with Children* is still treated in some quarters as if it were an underground mimeographed guideline instead of a modest official opening to the creation of genuine parochial worship. The clear directive that when a significant number of children are present at the *ordinary* Sunday celebration the prayers and readings may be modified accordingly is treated almost everywhere as too radical to be capable of implementation.

As long as it is considered a "violation of the rubrics" to omit a tertiary element of the Mass such as the Penitential Rite or the embolism after the Lord's prayer, the need to modify text is being treated with excessive timidity. It is a general fact of American Catholic life that we are willing to tolerate the verbosity of the Mass rite rather than modify it so we can pray appropriately. For example, experience shows readily that our Eucharistic Prayers are too long to be prayed and effectively heard with only three acclamations. We need either more acclamations or shorter prayers—and this is not simply a musical question. It is a serious liturgical question when the Eucharistic Prayer is supposed to be experienced as the prayer of the whole assembly (cf. No. 54 of the "General Instruction" of the Sacramentary). Similarly, the present Order of Mass is almost intolerably wordy under virtually all circumstances except those in which it can have the support of a full choir and a full complement of ministers. When we fail to modify the Mass rite for other circumstances, musical enhancement of a modest sort inevitably is experienced as a trivial appendage. *Music in Catholic Worship* all too timidly hints that this is the case, and we all too timidly approach this serious pastoral and liturgical matter.

Likewise (in No. 17), we are told (and who would disagree?) that "liturgical celebration presupposes a minimum of biblical knowledge and a deep commitment of living faith." On this principle, it makes no sense at all to accept the possibility that "lacking these conditions, the liturgy may be forced to become a tool of evangelization." Why? If the liturgy cannot be liturgy without faith, then least-common-denominator-please-everybody liturgies are at best inappropriate and possibly sacrilegious. The answer here is not to accept the liturgy's being forced into the mold of a tool for evangelization, but instead to create extraliturgical media for people who are unprepared for liturgy. It is time that we let the liturgy be liturgy and unbelievers be unbelievers and not try to force them together.

The document's treatment of "levels of faith" is disturbing, and the preoccupation with differences created by age is excessive and unbalanced. It would be more appropriate to consider styles rather than "levels" of faith. Otherwise, one is forced to conclude that those who can resonate with classic liturgical patterns (e.g., psalmody) necessarily have a "deeper" faith than those who thrive on

"Mother Dear, Oh Pray for Me." People and their ways of living their faith are simply much more complex than that. The document's formulation of the issue comes close to confusing "depth of faith" with "liturgical taste and level of theological education." In a world in which atheists can be moved to tears by the Jewish Kaddish *and* Gregorian chant, and liturgists can want both Amazing Grace *and* In Paradisum sung at their requiem (*I* do), the matter is much more complex than *Music in Catholic Worship* suggests.

The question of varied styles of living faith could be more constructively addressed. Current parish worship reflects a distinct tendency toward something like the old "High Mass, Low Mass" pattern, with one rather rich and elaborate Sunday Eucharist surrounded by a constellation of more modest celebrations. Rarely is this just a matter of "taste." Those who have strong investments in parochial or other aspects of Church life tend to gravitate to the "high" (actually often "folk") celebration, as those who have a lower churchly profile tend to gravitate to the "low." This pattern is especially evident in parishes where parish life is at its best—where there is an integrity about the way the Church's ministry is carried out.

Unfortunately, those who gravitate to the "Low Mass" celebration are too frequently and unfairly parodied as merely "getting in their obligation," and all to often what they get liturgically is a cut-down version (often watered-down) of what is done at the "high" celebration. They deserve better. The commitments of the "Low Mass" group are simply lived in a less churchly and explicit way, and from the perspective of their sober pieties, the "high" celebration frequently engaged in is showy and unnecessary (they will tell you it "takes too long"). Some of these people may simply be purchasing the cheapest possible fire insurance. Lest we be too fast to judge, however, few people with more conscious and articulate faith styles do what they do out of crystal pure love of God and neighbor. That the poor are always with us should not blind us to the work of the Spirit in the clotted clay that we all are.

The reform of the liturgy was aimed at a more communal and more explicit form of liturgical participation, and rightly so. But, equally important, the documents of Vatican II insist that the primary concern of Christians is the service of the Kingdom of God, not simply the building up of the Church. In may ways, those whose commitments are more in the world and less in the Church, and whose faith style is less articulate, may be standing on the cutting edge of that primary concern. We constantly attempt to evoke as an ideal a model of liturgical celebration that in fact only makes sense to those with a very high level of conscious and explicit churchly commitment. And this means that we give short shrift to celebrating appropriately the faith of those who stand in many ways at the cutting edge of the Church's real mission.

Most official directives (e.g., the official liturgical books) and most of the literature on liturgical celebration are actually oriented to the "high" style of celebration, or at least they make the most sense in that context. This means that the majority of American Catholic worshipers are left liturgical orphans. And the "Low Mass" celebrations in our churches painfully reflect this. Here, we need a less verbose Order of Mass and a kind of music suited to this sober and reticent faith style. We also need to develop fully communal feast day celebrations, preparing parishes in the Lent and Advent seasons to come together as one (i.e., in two or three co-equal and similar Eucharistic Liturgies).

Finally, the question of age differences needs another look. (It *is* a real question, as anyone knows who lives in a house where Billy Joel competes with Handel, with rare points of meeting around Neil Diamond). But the constant division into age groupings is a cultural sickness that the Church must grapple with in a wider context than the liturgical. For all the ecclesiastical rhetoric about the decline of the family, parochial lifestyle does little to promote the contact between the generations that family life is designed to serve. We will never grapple constructively with this question in liturgical celebration until we take a look at the way the Church lives and acts outside of times of celebration. As long as it constantly promotes separation between the ages and between the sexes in its programs and ministries, it will have a liturgical problem with age differences.

In sum, it is time that some significant footnotes to *Music in Catholic Worship* be grasped by the American Church. They should run something like this:

—The interface between text and music is so critical that, where necessary, liturgical texts must be modified in size, numbers and content just as song must be so modified according to the needs of specific groups and occasions;

—The *Directory for Masses with Children* should be taken seriously, but its general principles should be applied to other groups and occasions as well. Why should the children be the only special objects of the church's ministry?;

—There are a diversity of ways of living the Catholic faith, according to the gifts, opportunities and vocations of diverse Catholics. Liturgical celebration should reflect this diversity, and all expressions of faith should be cherished and nurtured. Concern for community should not become oppressive by the insistence that one *kind* of community style is normative for all Catholics; and

—Liturgical problems are often cultural problems. The Church should take care to discern what is good and what is damaging in the culture in which it is living. It should never accept cultural

presuppositions uncritically (e.g., uncritically accepting a generation gap).

Planning Feasts and Seasons

BY GABE HUCK

Gabe Huck is the Director of Liturgy Training Publications, Office for Divine Worship, Archdiocese of Chicago.

The two paragraphs on "The Occasion" in *Music in Catholic Worship* come as the second of three factors that must be considered in "planning pastoral celebrations" (*MCW* #14). They are placed between "The Congregation" and "The Celebrant." If planning as a whole is our concern, and not only music, this does not seem the most helpful grouping.

In the parish situation, those involved with liturgy must not forget about assembly and presider, but these are hardly fresh considerations every time there is planning to be done. Planners try to stay aware of the limitations of both these ministries, musically and otherwise, in a long process of training and freeing both to do the liturgy. They do the same for persons other than the presider who come from the assembly to take special ministries, musicians included. These are constants: no planning is done apart from the determination that some day it is going to be clear to all that the *assembly* celebrates the liturgy, and that presider and other special roles help this to happen. Planners may sometimes find it best to work on this a little at a time: to take on the problem of getting people to sit together this year, the improving of the presider's skills next, and to have definite steps toward the goals.

But in the ongoing task of planning for parish Sunday Eucharist, and for other liturgies, it is this middle element, "The Occasion," that deserves and takes the most effort. And how helpful is *MCW* here? Some of these ideas, reduced to a few words in the document, were and are wonderfully sensitive to the difficulties that have plagued planners. They point to an approach to the task that is far more realistic in terms of helping human beings pray together. Four of these ideas are well worth exploring: seasons as a basis for our planning, the spirit of feasts and seasons, the rhythm of the year, and the celebration that marks our Sunday.

First consider seasons as a basis for our planning. There is a presumption throughout these paragraphs that the seasons are fundamental in the work of planning and celebrating liturgy. This was not much heeded in 1972, nor since then. Two other approaches to parish liturgy still dominate. In the first, there is virtually no planning at all. Hymns are selected (for Masses with singing), the proper petitions and introductions are located in one of the "aids" available. This approach has little to do with the musical resources: it is as likely to happen in parishes with excellent choirs, good organists. Seasons happen only insofar as someone says, "Today is the second Sunday of Advent." They may then follow some suggestions of the missalette folk for song selection, but without any ability to integrate these into a season: there is nothing to integrate into.

The second, non-seasonal, approach usually involves people putting great hunks of time into planning Sunday by Sunday. In the extreme, this may mean occasionally tossing out the lectionary because something more immediate (the pastor's anniversary) needs to be celebrated. More likely, it means teams writing introductions, penance rites, petitions, after discovering the "theme" of the readings. When faced with Advent, the planners may impose one overall theme, *talking* it into the week-by-week liturgy. They thus recognize the existence of seasons, but only as artificial groupings of Sundays, which can receive any interpretation: "The theme of our advent liturgies this year is . . . ." A season is just an extended Sunday, one more unit, not related to what went before or what will follow. The sure sign that seasons themselves are not understood comes when Advent one year takes little or nothing from the previous year. It is created each year from nothing.

The document has only a fleeting sense for the importance of seasons. If only it had said something more: not so much a brief summary of each, but an acknowledgement that these carry—in their special words, sounds, movements—the only fully human way we have to ritualize our faith. Without such ritual, without ways to use all the senses and powers and feelings we have, things get stifling, things get boring. We receive faith, we hand on faith, not in creeds and commandments, but in the stories and songs and dances that come and go and return again in their various cycles. Only here do creeds and commandments and the way of living they aim to shape become part of a home, a place where I belong, somewhere I recognize. In the end, it is not that we practice the love of neighbor, not that we believe in the resurrection of the dead, that creates solidarity between us and with those before us: it is the way we have of affirming in ritual who we are and what we are about. For this to happen, we must not fear but respect repetition, for how else is the "me" of today tied to the "me" of yesterday and tomorrow? And we must see that seasons mean more than their Sunday gatherings: the ritual of a season is a whole. In Lent, it is not just six Sunday Eucharists, but the fasting and prayer and almsgiving, all expressing what our faith means, some vital part of it, with an intensity that can only be sustained these 40 days.

The finest line in these paragraphs is this: "Each feast and season has its own spirit and its own music." And this is where planners must begin. Not imposing a theme, but discovering a spirit. Too often we begin as if the season were something objective, sitting out there somewhere, a part of which each year we, the planners and homilists, want to clarify for the people. We act as if the Church invented these weeks just so as to clarify some particular point, to practice some specific discipline. So Advent becomes a meditation on the threefold coming of Christ, Easter an affirmation of faith that Jesus rose from the dead. We are over here, the season is over there, a thing to be approached, studied, perhaps even enjoyed.

But seasons are not primarily inventions for catechesis, nor mere historical commemorations, nor even the baptizing of the way our ancestors treated nature with a respect we lack. Before anything else, they are not out there, but inside us. They are human. They are people dealing with their humanity, with the most basic things they share with other people. Before it makes any sense to speak of Advent and the coming of Christ, Advent has to be experienced: the rites of December have to open our very own fears, our own feelings about time, our sense for what promise might mean. The planning of liturgy to keep an Advent does not begin in an overall theme and words for a banner; it begins with getting in touch with the Advent inside me, inside us.

So do we create Advent from nothing? This perhaps is the paradox. The more we recognize the way the season is human, that it is born in what short, dark days trigger in people, that whole facets of existence here need an Advent by any name to express themselves, then we see that Advent indeed can never be our own creation, but does have "its own spirit," which we hold in our hands. But it is a spirit, something elusive, never nailed down, never ever reduced to prose. Planners could begin with the time it takes to find some images of this spirit. It might be the colors that Advent suggests, that talk of darkness suggests, that talk of promise suggests. Read many of the Scriptures of Advent and talk about color, about texture. Is it rough or smooth, denim or silk, picket fence or barbed wire? Imagine Advent, image it. None are right, none wrong, but some will be more common, better images for the meanings Advent has in us. Such an approach is not easy for there is no power so subdued these days as our imaginations, that with which we need to do this imaging and then to bring it to effective ritual.

The special spirit of Advent naturally has a special music. Perhaps somebody captured a bit of this in the melody of "O Come, O Come, Emmanuel," and somebody else in "Wake, Awake" and somebody more recently in "When from Our Exile." But to begin, it can be good just to think of the sound of Advent. Actual sounds: snow falls, spinning tires, department stores, Santa with his bell. And music that seems to contain the images of Advent. Maybe that's the sound of some rock group, or a folk ballad, a bit of jazz. Maybe it is a certain tempo. Maybe it is a particular instrument. The point is not that somehow these sounds are going to become a part of the advent liturgy, but that they are images of Advent itself. Beyond that, they do begin to suggest what Advent can sound like. And they also might suggest the idea of progression, movement within the season itself, and growth into Christmas.

All this imaging brings first a sense for the spirit of a season, then, slowly, how the ritual can express some of this for us. Most often, this will not be a matter of wordy explanations or of unique gestures or objects or drama that are for this year only. Most often, rather, it will be asking, for example: How can the Entrance Rite draw the mood of this season about us, an environment for our prayer? What will be the movement? What use of silence? posture? lighting? song? words? gestures? What is the pace of this rite? Will this Entrance Rite be the same each Sunday or will it change slightly? It will also mean asking whether or not there can be some time to bring the lectors together to share something of the spirit of the season and to discuss how the Scriptures are the very source of that spirit and the difference they as lectors can make. It will mean considering the seasonal use of a Responsorial Psalm, one that will be known by heart the second or third time through. It will mean selecting acclamations that have the sound of the season, or accompanying the usual acclamation in a way that will help them take on this sound.

When planners approach a season in this way, knowing how human and how personal the season is and yet how they are to respect its special spirit, they have set themselves for a long-range work. Only by letting the good things happen year after year, which requires good records and good evaluations, will their work bear fruit. Each season will become familiar, will be freed to speak for, speak to, each person and the community as they are this particular year.

The document notes that penitential occasions demand more restraint, great feasts more solemnity; also that people will want to sing more on the feasts and less during the ordinary time. We can take this as an illustration of the respect planners need for the cycle, the rhythm of the year as well as an indication for the ways the cycle is perceived by its celebrants. The great tragedy of the leveling of the seasons that has happened since Vatican II has been the loss of the yearly rhythm that was at least captured by the existence of a definite Lent, with disciplines and liturgies, and various seasonal devotions (Mary in May, the dead during November, etc.). Apart from any ecclesiastical or theological considerations, we humans need a rhythm of greater and lesser, of anticipation and celebration; we need the special times and the ordinary times, and all kinds of moods within the special days. We have not outgrown this for there is nothing immature about it.

The great problem here, the one we will be dealing with for generations perhaps, is how this sense for seasons and their rhythm can be maintained when the culture lives by quite other values and rituals. Perhaps we need patience most as we work with liturgy, and a sense of proportion.

The document speaks of what makes solemnity: "less the ornateness of song and magnificence of ceremonial" than "worthy and religious celebration." Yes, but what prompts worthy and religious celebration, the kind that is so special it can only come a few times a year? Trying to do it only with special pieces by the choir, new banners and so on only communicates information and perhaps provides spectator enjoyment to the assembly. Solemnity just does not happen apart from anticipation, and this is exactly what the rhythm of seasons can create, especially as it sinks into us through the years. A good Christmas liturgy is possible because of a good Advent. A good Easter and Eastertime liturgy can happen when there is a real Lent. Even so, those who plan the great feasts need to know that if they have created anticipation, then they must allow for expression at the solemnity, that people will not be satisfied with listening and holding still, that the acclamations and hymns of the assembly are not to be given to the choir. The challenge is for a sense of what solemnity feels like to those who have anticipated and whose ministry is to be the assembly. There is also real need to provide for flexibility in the length of these liturgies.

The document speaks also of another kind of solemnity, the "important event in family and parish life." Here also we are dealing with rhythms: not only the annual parish cycle of first communions, adult initiation and the like, but the life cycle itself: weddings, funerals and such are great solemnities for those present and deserve the best efforts of the parish community.

More could have been said of the celebration of Sunday. "Sundays will be celebrated with variety but always as befits the day of the Lord." What does befit the day of the Lord? So many of our failures these years come from basic neglect of the Sunday Eucharist, neglect simply to make it good ritual. Those who do care too often have not seen what sort of thing we are doing on Sunday when we meet to pray and instead have imposed their own visions and fancies.

But Sunday by Sunday we gather to tell some part of our story, to reflect on it, and then to bless and share the bread and wine. It is a simple sort of thing, powerful when the flow of the rite is respected. Music within this rite is not hard, is not optional, is not up for grabs. It is how we do the rite; it marks the rhythm. For the most part, it is not something that we need to find or follow in shabby booklets or in beautiful hymnals: if this rite marks every seventh day for us through a year, most of its melodies are known by heart. They flow through the rite, not with a sense of "Now we will stop everything and sing," but with a sense of things fitting well together.

This day of the Lord, Sunday, this regular coming together of the assembly, is how the Church has songs to sing and so how it continues to live. It is our songs that don't stop at the church doors, that can be a vocabulary for family or friends or an individual to make Eucharist, thanksgiving, all day long and all life long. Each Sunday is to make the song stronger.

The Celebrant Must Be There

BY RITA CLARE DORNER AND ANNE MARIE MONGOVEN

Sr. Rita Claire Dorner, OP is currently completing a degree in liturgical studies at Catholic University. Sr. Anne Marie Mongoven, OP is currently a doctoral candidate in cathechetics at this same university.

The house lights dim. The audience is hushed. The conductor steps on the podium. All is in readiness for the concert to begin. The adequacy or inadequacy, the success or failure of the musical rendition is in the hands of the conductor.

Who is the conductor? S/he is the one who presides at the concert. It is his/her task to draw from the musicians the sound and the performance that will successfully interpret the composer's score. The obvious role is one of leadership. S/he unifies the orchestra by setting the tempo, calling for particular dynamics of sound, determining the style and technique of each piece.

But the performance is the end product of the conductor's work. The task begins with planning as s/he selects the compositions to be performed, rehearses with the musicians, and helps them to interpret the music.

Each composition performed is affected by the attitude, style and bearing of the conductor. S/he brings his/her own technique, education, experience and uniqueness. The style of conducting is characterized by the use of the baton, the gestures and body movement, the eye contact with the members of the orchestra. The rapport with each musician and with the orchestra as a whole is vital to the functioning of the group as a unit.

The presider at liturgy is not unlike a conductor. His orchestra is the entire worshiping community. He unifies, leads, sets the tempo, interprets and determines the style of celebration. If he is to be a successful conductor, his work must also include planning, rehearsing and study. A good presider is the *sine qua non* of good liturgical celebration.

"No other factor," says *Music in Catholic Worship*, "affects the liturgy as much as the attitude, style, and bearing of the celebrant." The statement goes on to describe his attitude, style and bearing as being "his sincere faith and warmth as he welcomes the worshiping community; his human naturalness combined with dignity and seriousness as he breaks the Bread of Word and Eucharist." What is meant by attitude, style, bearing and human naturalness? Is it possible to consider these factors when planning liturgies?

The word "style" often conjures up the idea of something put on, an unnatural way of acting. The fact is that everyone has a style. No presider is without one. It may be affective, condescending, inobtrusive, quiet, exaggerated, relaxed, unselfconscious, proprietary, friendly, withdrawn, mechanical, indecisive or hospitable. It may express isolation or relationship. Style is always present and it speaks loudly and clearly to the assembled community.

Style is expressed in the way the presider enters into the liturgical action. Is he enthusiastic or mechanical? Enthusiasm does not have to be exuberant; a quiet enthusiasm communicates as well as exuberance. Is he respectful, reverent toward all other ministers, including the community? This reverence is expressed in his posture, his voice, through hands and gesture and eyes.

The presider's bearing is a part of his style. Does he look at those to whom he speaks? Is he obviously listening when others are speaking? When he handles the book or the bread and wine, or when he greets the people are reverence and sincerity visible? A perfunctory greeting or impatient waiting are manifested not only in voice, but also in bearing.

The presider's attitude cannot be hidden. The attitude in question is the attitude he has toward what he is doing and toward the community he is leading. His task is one of "breaking the Bread of Word and Eucharist." Does he believe he is doing this task *with* the community or *for* them? Does he believe he is serving the community and that the community is also serving him? Does he believe the liturgical action is a celebration of the faith of the whole community? These beliefs express themselves in an attitude toward what he is doing and the people with whom he is doing it. The presider is terribly vulnerable, for he cannot hide his attitudes.

The presider at liturgy is asked to possess a "human naturalness combined with dignity and seriousness." Human naturalness is different in each human being. One person is gregarious, another withdrawn. One is relaxed, another cautious. Naturalness is expressed in showing what is real. The personality of the presider cannot be constructed to match some nebulous ideal. The presider must be free to express in his own natural way his deep faith and his profound love of the community.

Every liturgical celebration cannot be a high emotional peak, not even for the presider. We all grow weak and tired and our enthusiasm is eroded by our weariness. But feeling profoundly the need to celebrate our faith in sign and symbol and ritual play, we come together to worship. The presider who can lift us out of our lethargy by the warmth of his welcome, by the sincerity of his faith, by the joy that he manifests in being with us and for us—this presider, through his human naturalness, his attitude, style and bearing, is a person we cannot do without.

Should these qualities of the presider be considered by the liturgy team as it plans the parish celebrations? If we are willing to face it, the question is: can they *not* be part of that planning? If no other single factor affects the liturgy as much as the presider, is it unfair to him to leave him isolated while he bears such a responsibility? Certainly some of those who presently act as president of the assembly are not ready to ask for such help. Perhaps sensitively and gently, as the liturgical team assists the other ministers, it may begin to strengthen and sustain the presider by leading him to consider these aspects of his own ministry.

MCW singles out one fact of the presider's overall stance at worship—his role as a singer. Commenting on this role, it states that music should "facilitate the effectiveness of a good celebrant." Are celebrants aware that music contributes to their overall effectiveness? If so, how much planning, thought and time are given to this aspect of the presider's role?

Recognizing that music enhances the spoken word, solemnizes it, and lends it beauty, the presider knows that whenever words are sung and sung well, these words come to life in a new way. Then what words should be sung? Since it has been recommended that the people sing their acclamations, the most obvious parts for the celebrant to sing are the parts that lead into the sung acclamations: the preface, the introduction to the anamnesis, the doxology leading to the Great Amen. The dialogue between presider and people is enhanced when the words are sung in a vigorous way. The music in the sacramentary contains many options for all these parts. Perhaps during the next decade composers will provide additional settings with a more contemporary sound.

The presider as a member of the community enhances the feeling of unity and solidarity with all present when he sings with the people whenever possible. The celebrant who enters the church in procession with the other ministers, carrying his hymn book and singing, immediately sets up a feeling of "We're all worshiping together; we are one united people."

What if the presider cannot sing or cannot sing well? MCW states that "if capable of singing, he ought, for the sake of people, to rehearse carefully the sung parts that would contribute to their celebration." The key word is "rehearse." Do presiders spend time rehearsing? Could the choir director's job description include weekly sessions with celebrants to help them sing entrance and recessional hymns, the dialogue and proclamation parts of the liturgy, and to offer them suggestions for vocal improvement?

MCW notes that what the presider "cannot sing well and effectively he ought to recite" (No. 22). Have we tended to use this statement as a loophole that excuses the presider from singing at all? All presiders are not great singers, but a liturgical celebration is not a concert. If singing enhances the celebration, does not the presider have an obligation "for the sake of people" to sing whenever possible? "The priest who will first rehearse what he must sing honors the community for whom he celebrates and shows the seriousness with which he treats his sacerdotal ministry" (Lucien Deiss, *Spirit and Song of the New Liturgy*, p. 29).

Music in Catholic Worship: Section III

THE PLACE OF MUSIC IN THE CELEBRATION

THE PLACE OF MUSIC IN THE CELEBRATION

Music Serves the Expression of Faith

23. Among the many signs and symbols used by the Church to celebrate its faith, music is of preeminent importance. As sacred song united to words it forms a necessary or a integral part of the solemn liturgy.[10] Yet the function of music is ministerial; it must serve and never dominate. Music should assist the assembled believers to express and share the gift of faith that is within them and to nourish and strengthen their interior commitment of faith. It should heighten the texts so that they speak more fully and more effectively. The quality of joy and enthusiasm which music adds to community worship cannot be gained in any other way. It imparts a sense of unity to the congregation and sets the appropriate tone for a particular celebration.

24. In addition to expressing texts, music can also unveil a dimension of meaning and feeling, a communication of ideas and intuitions which words alone cannot yield. This dimension is integral to the human personality and to growth in faith. It cannot be ignored if the signs of worship are to speak to the whole person. Ideally, every communal celebration of faith, including funerals and the sacraments of baptism, confirmation, penance, anointing, and matrimony, should include music and singing. Where it is possible to celebrate the Liturgy of the Hours in a community, it, too, should include music.

25. To determine the value of a given musical element in a liturgical celebration a threefold judgment must be made: musical, liturgical, and pastoral.

The Musical Judgment

26. Is the music technically, aesthetically, and expressively good? This judgment is basic and primary and should be made by competent musicians. Only artistically sound music will be effective in the long run. To admit the cheap, the trite, the musical cliche often found in popular songs for the purpose of "instant liturgy" is to cheapen the liturgy, to expose it to ridicule, and to invite failure.

27. Musicians must search for and create music of quality for worship, especially the new musical settings for the new liturgical texts. They must also do the research needed to find new uses for the best of the old music. They must explore the repertory of good music used in other communions. They must find practical means of preserving and using our rich heritage of Latin chants and motets.[11]

In the meantime, however, the words of St. Augustine should not be forgotten: "Do not allow yourselves to be offended by the imperfect while you strive for the perfect.

28. We do a disservice to musical values, however, when we confuse the judgment of music with the judgment of musical style. Style and value are two distinct judgments. Good music of new styles is finding a happy home in the celebrations of today. To chant and polyphony we have effectively added the chorale hymn, restored responsorial singing to some extent, and employed many styles of contemporary composition. Music in folk idiom is finding acceptance in eucharistic celebrations. We must judge value within each style.

"In modern times the Church has consistently recognized and freely admitted the use of various styles of music as an aid to liturgical worship. Since the promulgation of the Constitution on the Liturgy and more especially since the introduction of vernacular languages into the liturgy, there has arisen a more pressing need for musical compositions in idioms that can be sung by the congregation and thus further communal participation."[12]

29. The musician has every right to insist that the music be good. But although all liturgical music should be good music, not all good music is suitable to the liturgy. The

musical judgment is basic but not final. There remain the liturgical and pastoral judgments.

The Liturgical Judgments

30. The nature of the liturgy itself will help to determine what kind of music is called for, what parts are to be preferred for singing and who is to sing them.

a. STRUCTURAL REQUIREMENTS

31. The choice of sung parts, the balance between them and the style of musical setting used should reflect the relative importance of the parts of the Mass (or other service) and the nature of each part. Thus elaborate settings of the entrance song, "Lord have Mercy" and "Glory to God" may make the proclamation of the word seem unimportant; an overly elaborate offertory song with a spoken "Holy, Holy, Holy Lord" may make the eucharistic prayer seem less important.

b. TEXTUAL REQUIREMENTS

32. Does the music express and interpret the text correctly and make it more meaningful? Is the form of the text respected? In making these judgments the principal classes of texts must be kept in mind: proclamations, acclamations, psalms and hymns, and prayers. Each has a specific function which must be served by the music chosen for a text.

In most instances there is an official liturgical text approved by the episcopal conference. "Vernacular texts set to music composed in earlier periods," however, "may be used in liturgical texts."[13] As noted elsewhere, criteria have been provided for the texts which may replace the processional chants of Mass. In these cases and in the choice of all supplementary music, the texts "must always be in conformity with Catholic doctrine; indeed they should be drawn chiefly from holy scripture and from liturgical sources."[14]

c. ROLE DIFFERENTIATION

33. "In liturgical celebrations each one, minister or layperson, who has an office to perform, should do all of, but only, those parts which pertain to that office by the nature of the rite and the principles of liturgy."[15] Special musical concern must be given to the roles of the congregation, the cantor, the choir, and the instrumentalists.

d. THE CONGREGATION

34. Music for the congregation must be within its members' performance capability. The congregation must be comfortable and secure with what they are doing in order to celebrate well.

e. THE CANTOR

35. While there is no place in the liturgy for display of virtuosity for its own sake, artistry is valued, and an individual singer can effectively lead the assembly, attractively proclaim the Word of God in the psalm sung between the readings, and take his or her part in other responsorial singing. "Provision should be made for at least one or two properly trained singers, especially where there is no possibility of setting up even a small choir. The singer will present some simpler musical settings, with the people taking part, and can lead and support the faithful as far as is needed. The presence of such a singer is desirable even in churches which have a choir, for those celebrations in which the choir cannot take part but which may fittingly be performed with some solemnity and therefore with singing."[16] Although a cantor "cannot enhance the service of worship in the same way as a choir, a trained and competent cantor can perform an important ministry by leading the congregation in common sacred song and in responsorial singing."[17]

f. THE CHOIR

36. A well-trained choir adds beauty and solemnity to the liturgy and also assists and encourages the singing of the congregation. The Second Vatican Council, speaking of the choir, stated emphatically: "Choirs must be diligently promoted," provided that "the whole body of the faithful may be able to contribute that active participation which is rightly theirs."[18]

"At times the choir, within the congregation of the faithful and as part of it, will assume the role of leadership, while at other times it will retain its own distinctive ministry. This means that the choir will lead the people in sung prayer, by alternating or reinforcing the sacred song of the congregation, or by enhancing it with the addition of a musical elaboration. At other times in the course of liturgical celebration the choir alone will sing works whose musical demands enlist and challenge its competence."[19]

g. THE ORGANIST AND OTHER INSTRUMENTALISTS

37. Song is not the only kind of music suitable for liturgical celebration. Music performed on the organ and other instruments can stimulate feelings of joy and contemplation at appropriate times.[20] This can be done effectively at the following points: an instrumental prelude, a soft background to a spoken psalm, at the preparation of the gifts in place of singing, during portions of the communion rite, and the recessional.

In the dioceses of the United States, "musical instruments other than the organ may be used in liturgical services, provided they are played in a manner that is suitable to public worship."[21] This decision deliberately refrains from singling out specific instruments. Their use depends on circumstances, the nature of the congregation, etc.

38. The *proper placing* of the organ and choir according to the arrangement and acoustics of the church will facilitate celebration. Practically speaking, the choir must be near the director and the organ (both console and sound). The choir ought to be able to perform without too much distraction; the acoustics ought to give a lively presence of sound in the choir area and allow both tone and word to reach the congregation with clarity. Visually it is desirable that the choir appear to be part of the worshipping community, yet a part which serves in a unique way. Locating the organ console too far from the congregation causes a time lag which tends to make the singing drag unless the organist is trained to cope with it. A location near the front pews will facilitate congregational singing.

The Pastoral Judgment

39. The pastoral judgment governs the use and function of every element of celebration. Ideally this judgment is made by the planning team or committee. It is the judgment that must be made in this particular situation, in these concrete circumstances. Does music in the celebration enable these people to express their faith, in this place, in this age, in this culture?

40. The instruction of the Congregation for Divine Worship, issued September 5, 1970, encourages episcopal conferences to consider not only liturgical music's suitability to the time and circumstances of the celebration, "but also the needs of the faithful who will sing them. All means must be used to promote singing by the people. New forms should be used, which are adapted to the different mentalities and to modern tastes." The document adds that the music and the instruments "should correspond to the sacred character of the celebration and the place of worship."

41. A musician may judge that a certain composition or style of composition is good music but his musical judgment really says nothing about whether and how this music is to be used in this celebration. The signs of the celebration must be accepted and received as meaningful for a genuinely human faith experience for these specific worshippers. This pastoral judgment can be aided by sensitivity to the cultural and social characteristics of the people who make up the congregation: their age, culture, and education. These factors influence the effectiveness of the liturgical signs, including music. No set of rubrics or regulations of itself will ever achieve a truly pastoral celebration of the sacramental rites. Such regulations must always be applied with a pastoral concern for the given worshipping community.

Is It Any Good?
The Musical Judgment

BY EDWARD GUTFREUND

Mr. Gutfreund is a parish musician, composer, folk artist and author in Cincinnati, Oh.

Judging is difficult and in many ways unfashionable in this time. Accepting everything without evaluation is proposed as another way of respecting the individual and allowing each person maximum freedom. Nevertheless, technical skills and expertise that the musician acquires can be offered as liturgy is prepared. Taking advantage of these skills can eliminate learning everything by experience.

I am frequently reminded of a plaque I once saw: "Learn from other people's mistakes. You can't live long enough to make them all yourself." Music as an art and a skill is refined enough to make it possible to avoid mistakes beforehand. Using good musical principles will also offer springboards from which we may move to new areas of discovery. We have a wealth of musical heritage as a Church. Its power will no doubt push us forward in that search. How much is there yet to be heard?

Music in Catholic Worship raises questions and gives some direction. Years of living with the document have generated experience that expands those sections. It makes demands about quality—technical, aesthetic and expressive quality—and invites criticism about the artistic form and structure of the music. (Nos. 26–28). These sections raise very important questions about style (we have seen many styles of musicianship and song leading in the years of liturgical renewal). Little is said, however, concerning the musician's role in using music. Little is said about taking good quality music and performing it badly. Nothing is said about misrepresenting the created form of the music by inaccurate and unthoughtful performance. Nor is anything said about creative use and arrangements of music that may on first sight appear elementary or even trite. More needs to be said concerning an integration of musical tone or mood with the needed tone or mood of a given liturgical moment.

The threefold judgment concerning the technical, aesthetic and expressive qualities of a piece of music is perhaps the strongest and most helpful statement in this section; for if we examine these qualities of a piece of music, we will be familiar with the form of the music and thus with some of the corresponding potential uses within the liturgy. (From the outset this process implies a way of integrating the liturgical and pastoral judgments.)

"Is the music technically good"—correct, clear, and in complete musical structure and form? Do the melodies and harmonies work well together? Do the accents and rhythms fit with the text and vice versa? Are the phrases, periods and sections in good relationship to one another? Without proper technical qualities, a song will not work. Rough edges or holes in the music will cause distraction, insecurity, and frustration for the people who listen or sing it. Similar problems occur if a correct piece of music is performed inaccurately.

"Is the piece *aesthetically* good"—pleasing, captivating, provocative, engaging? Will the musician and congregation have the potential for experiencing more than simply the stimulation of the aural faculty? Can the music provide something beyond sound or a cover for action or an unwanted silence?

"Is the music *expressively* good"—dynamic, emphatic, suggestive, coherent, clear? Does the music have the potential for expressing a given text or a needed mood for the liturgy? Does it say something and speak a portion of the faith we attempt to communicate to one another in our liturgy?

Choosing music that has been evaluated from these three points of view will bring us to the conclusion made in the document that "only artistically sound music will be effective in the long run." Making these judgments will quickly eliminate what is referred to as "the cheap or the trite."

It seems however, that our increased experience and experimentation does challenge a portion of the final sentence (No. 26). If the section implies that all popular music is necessarily musical cliche, I would take issue with it. Granted, to attempt instantly successful liturgy by "putting on a good show" does potentially cheapen the liturgy. However, the quantity and quality of popular music has expanded to such an amazing degree that we would do well to learn its secret of captivating audiences and providing powerful musical experience rather than to imply that popular music is necesssarily bad music. The use of popular music in the liturgy is its own complicated question more appropriately discussed under the pastoral judgment (Nos. 39–41). But the quality of music that is readily available to us in this greatly electronic age is worth attending to. It offers one more way to increase our understanding of music as an art form.

It also tells us something about people's ability to learn. It is not at all surprising to find people from very young to very old who are most at ease singing complicated rhythm and melody structures that have become popular through the media. It is not always a question of difficulty that keeps people from participating. They learn the things that capture their attention or provide significant experiences. Perhaps we shortchange them by always looking for songs that are easy to learn. Congregations who are helped to learn difficult pieces sing them better, and the songs last longer than the elementary music frequently offered. Once again, as is so often necessary, we are looking to balance variety, freshness, stability and longevity in our pastoral choices. Composers can be stirred by these challenges—as well as frequently frustrated in their attempts to discern and respond to congregational needs.

Music in Catholic Worship (No. 27) encourages us to "search for and create music of quality for worship." Many of the new liturgical texts provide qualities of rise and fall in celebrations. If well done, rising and falling dynamics are productive. If accidental and if things are not done well, the event is a failure. When evaluating the music for new texts, we must look hard at the earlier statement (No. 26), particularly at whether the music is expressively good. The Responsorial Psalm, Alleluia and eucharistic acclamations deserve much more attention than is usually given. They are different musically as well as textually. It often seems that these are chosen because they are needed structurally and are not sufficiently evaluated musically.

We are encouraged to examine our connection to the past. Much remains to be done in this area, for on different days we have either sanctified the treasures of the old or abandoned them with disdain. Neither approach reflects balance, reality or respect.

We are also encouraged to examine our ecumenical relationships, to draw on the wisdom of other traditions and denominations. This seems to be occurring both in choirs working together and in the many prayer communities that are interdenominational.

A quote from St. Augustine offers tremendous encouragement to temper our strong sense of trying too hard. Rereading this quote regularly would help us maintain sanity in our pilgrimaging toward effective worship: "Do not allow yourself to be offended by the imperfect while you strive for the perfect." Because we have been willing to work long and hard in our imperfection, we are making progress. It is no doubt never fast enough to suit us, but neither is the arrival of the kingdom.

The continuous stamina of the many parish musicians I have met is a great source of optimism. All we have at present is the imperfect, yet it has potential to move us toward the perfect. For our lives as pastoral musicians, this process is the best we can hope for. Progress can be made when we take on the imperfect and work with it, rather than allowing the imperfect to numb us, to numb our sensitivities, and therefore dampen our eagerness to keep searching. In spite of our well-thought-out principles and theories, much real growth is occurring in our people and in communities that are using very imperfect means.

Music in Catholic Worship, then, speaks of clarifying the difference between musical value and musical style. Again there is the potential conflict between professional expertise and subjective taste. It is too easy to remember strong comments made about the "crummy organ music" or the "disrespectful folk group." The comments often come from inclinations to different styles rather than from real judgment of musical quality. A hopeful development these days is the joining of styles within celebrations. Many parishes are seeing the value of incorporating the folk group with the traditional choir and attempting to prepare celebrations that reflect the great pluralism of our communities. The document simply says we must judge value within each style. The difficulty that has often arisen is to equate value with style.

Because my experience is primarily in the folk idiom, it is apparent that more than one sentence would be called for about the idiom. Obviously, the folk idiom has moved to a position far beyond that of "finding acceptance." Many good influences have arisen out of the developments of the folk idiom in recent years. Because the style often includes different levels of formality and sometime different theological emphases, there has been a broadening in liturgical practice.

When I see the 75–100 people who attend regular Folk Musicians' Forum meetings in our diocese, and when I meet many other musicians throughout the country, I am convinced that there is a great desire to know musical quality and to provide effective, exciting and inspiring pastoral worship. The simple role of leading folk songs has expanded to responsibilities of nearly orchestral proportions. The lone guitarist/cantor is now usually part of a folk ensemble and choir. The idiom is far from fading out of existence. There are some moments when all of us wish that simple organ accompaniment would expand to similar proportions.

The long-standing axiom *Degustibus non disputandum esse* reminds us that taste (and here we include style) is not to be disputed. *Music in Catholic Worship*, however, as well as our eagerness for good liturgy, both remind us that whatever style is chosen deserves to be done well. It deserves to be done in such a way that people experience the power of music, the power that can communicate and stimulate the whole range of emotions and ideas, as well as prepare the ground for a most receptive awareness of the good news.

Does It Fit?
The Liturgical Judgment

BY JOSEPH CUNNINGHAM

Rev. Joseph Cunningham is Principal of Cathedral Preparatory Seminary and former Executive Secretary of the Diocesan Liturgical Commission, Brooklyn, N.Y.

There is a liturgical need to define more specifically the kinds of prayers in ritual celebrations. The kind of prayer determines musical style. We are most aware of this principle in music for acclamations: Alleluia, Holy, eucharistic acclamation and Amen. What most parishes sing weekly are melodies that are musically best for the acclamatory parts of the liturgy. Hundreds have been written but few are sung. Unless the composer clearly grasps the genre of the text, even fine music may never do what it is supposed to do. An acclamation in worship is no different in kind from the song "Happy Birthday To You." It is *always* sung with a very simple repetitive melody. Acclamations in the Mass must have this same spontaneity and familiarity in their musical structures, thus enabling them to always be sung. A judgment is necessary for determining a particular choice. A masterful piece of music for an acclamatory text, if it is not written in the proper style, should rightly be rejected on the basis of liturgical inappropriateness.

Concern for the whole structure of the liturgy (whether eucharistic or other rituals) is part of liturgical judgment. *Music in Catholic Worship* emphasizes the imbalance that results from a totally sung Rite of Entrance. From the liturgical point of view there are many other concerns to be considered in planning each celebration.

The Entrance Rite calls the assembly together with a readiness to pray and directs all to the Proclamation of the Word. In effect, the presider is saying: "Folks, we are all here for a purpose; let us begin by listening to the Word of God." A proper proportion of music, depending on the occasion, enables this to happen well.

The Responsorial Psalm is a refrain with psalm verses to aid understanding of the texts read. A meditative form of prayer, it should not tax the energy level of the congregation.

Proclamation is the genre of the Word itself. On some special occasions the gospel reading might be sung by the deacon with a chant or contemporary melody, but the message must come through clearly. Readings are usually proclaimed best by reading them distinctly.

The structure of the Preparation of the Gifts is a matter for careful liturgical judgment. What are we doing at this point? The celebrant presides over the collecting of gifts from the entire congregation (collection), prepares and designates some bread and wine as the elements for this Mass. It is a relatively minor and transitional part of the Mass. Having heard the Word of God, we pause to think about its effect in our lives as we prepare to share in Jesus' work of saving us. Liturgical understanding of structure determines musical choice: first whether music is necessary at all; second, the type of song; and third, who should do it.

The Communion Rite, on the popular level, has become very confusing musically. The Lamb of God is an important song to accompany the Breaking of Bread, but it has very often become overshadowed by a song of peace at the exchange. Liturgical judgment causes us to recognize that we do not need a song to duplicate what each person is expressing to another person nearby. We simply exchange a ritual gesture expressing reconciliation and unity and proceed with the Breaking of Bread and the reception of Eucharist.

Procession is the ritual prayer in which the community is involved as each receives the Eucharist. All parades or processions (religious parades) need music. Pastoral experience and judgments point out two problems that must be taken into consideration by liturgists and musicians: first, people do not always sing best at this time; second, with Communion in the hand as an option, holding a hymnal will be difficult. On the basis of liturgical requirements we should not abandon a congregational song but urge musicians to use variety with instruments, cantors and choir, and simple refrains for the congregation, during this very important procession.

In other sacraments, liturgical structures must be respected musically. In the marriage ceremony, it is poor liturgy to interrupt the ritual after the exchange of marriage vows and before the blessing of rings for a song of thanksgiving. The exchange of rings (while somewhat anticlimactic and repetitive of the verbal exchange) is a ritual action full of meaning, which, after a long song, becomes totally disconnected. A spontaneous acclamation by way of applause might be quite appropriate here, instead of a scheduled song of thanks.

In Baptism and Confirmation, the presiding minister says: "This is our faith, this is the faith of the Church, we are proud to profess it in Christ Jesus, Our Lord." Song by way of acclamation that says loudly, "Yes we believe and we are glad" is called for.

The rite of Christian burial calls for faith-motivated joy tempered by human sadness. A funeral is not a "Mass of Resurrection," as it was popularly called. Nor does the ritual reflect all the joy that is ours at Easter. Thus, sensitive liturgical judgment based on the true intention of the ritual must be exercised over the musical selections.

If we expect people to be serious about worship, we have to be very concerned about the texts we ask them to sing. One of the most jarring obstacles to prayer is to be forced to say something that is incorrect or ungrammatical, or that reflects a type of piety that one does not personally hold. It can be embarrassing at a Saturday evening Mass to sing "...early in the morning our prayers shall rise to Thee"; or during the preparation of the gifts to sing "...for when the sacred words are done..."; or reflecting on human dignity "...that saved a wretch like me..."

Some of the more archaic texts reproduced in some recent hymnals are a distraction to prayer rather than a help (especially when a community knows the same melody with better, albeit not the original, words). Obviously, prayer appreciates poetic license expecially in song texts, but the movement should be toward current language.

Pastors and musicians have seen the value in maintaining some Latin songs in a parish repertoire. Chant versions of the *Sanctus*, *Agnus Dei* and the *Kyrie* have been highly beneficial for people in their prayer, expecially since they fully understand what they are singing. From an educational point of view it seems it was necessary to move completely into the vernacular before we were able to know that at specific times and circumstances Latin still has its place.

For too long we have been lamenting the fact that Catholic people do not sing well. We have noted that the Protestant tradition has maintained song in worship and as a result has a good corpus of music (which until recently we have not shared). It is time to stop and listen to the present Roman Catholic congregations at worship. People are in fact singing, and in many cases they are singing well. We would not have the copyright problem emerging or the publication of so many new hymnals if song were not becoming an established imperative in congregational prayer life.

While *Music in Catholic Worship* defines the cantor's role very well, the place of the emerging leader of song is left undefined and uncertain. Many parishes find that they cannot get congregations to sing with the professional artist; sometimes the cantor is too good or so overpowering that he or she is listened to, but not responded to. In some parishes, there are so many Masses every Sunday that a professional cannot come to all of them. For reasons such as these, parishioners are timidly coming forward as leaders of song, and are allowing their voices, over a microphone, to support the congregation. They do not have the strength or the confidence of the professional cantor, yet their presence is necessary to encourage congregational singing. Leaders of song should never be untrained but nor do they have to be professionals. The gradations of involvement in fulfilling this role should be accepted, encouraged and better defined in revised versions of the document.

The pendulum swing regarding choirs is typical of many aspects of worship. No document connected with the liturgical reform stated that choirs were to be phased out of existence, but two things have led to their diminished prominence: an all-or-nothing approach on the part of choir members, who often had an instant dislike for liturgical reform including vernacular and communal song, and thought it their innate right to sing everything they sang before the reform; and a misguided curtailment of the choir's role by those who sought their help to support unison congregational song or syphoned off individual members to be leaders of song.

As we reexamine the place of music in our worship we do so with much more balance. Choirs should be encouraged to maintain the chant and polyphonic traditions so dear to the Church for centuries. Young people have not heard these in many parishes, and older people long for them. Chant and polyphony are wedded to the Latin language and have a valid place in worship as motets, meditation songs and even congregational singing where possible. On the other hand, choirs should undertake descants and harmonies accompanying congregational hymns. Many of the better hymnals publish choir editions.

The location of organ consoles in churches has gone through the phase (and craze) similar to that of the crying room. During one period, every new church had a crying room. They have since been abandoned, not because the babies that once inhabited them on Sundays grew up, but because they did not serve their purpose well. The same is true of the movement of the organ console from the choir loft to the front of a church in renovated interiors. This has not always been a satisfactory solution. Designers, liturgical consultants and musicians should be involved in the discussion of the location of the organ console in each situation as well as the proper design of the organ for the interior spaces of a church. Replacing a pipe organ in need of extensive repair with an inadequate but cheap electronic instrument (as has happened too often) is a severe disservice to the ministry of music. Congregational song will never be satisfactory under these conditions.

Everyone agrees that *Music in Catholic Worship* is a remarkable pastoral document that properly interprets both musical and liturgical principles for practical use. Because of its widespread study by worshiping communities, both its wisdom and some shortcomings can be pointed out. Looking at the document after ten years is a good decision, and any attempt to adjust sections of its contents cannot help but enhance our ministry of music in worship.

COMMENTARY ON 39–41

Will It Work?
The Pastoral Judgment

BY VIRGIL C. FUNK

Rev. Virgil C. Funk is president of the National Association of Pastoral Musicians.

Of the three judgments for church music (musical, liturgical, pastoral), the pastoral judgment is the most sophisticated, intangible, crucial and elusive. Perhaps this is why, of the three judgments given in *Music in Catholic Worship*, least is said about the pastoral judgment!

The pastoral judgment is concerned not simply with principles, but with implementation, with specific situations and everyday people, with boring celebrants and temperamental musicians, with early-morning liturgies and acoustically dead church buildings—and with a few crying kids thrown in.

The pastoral judgment, says *Music in Catholic Worship*, is primary and governs every aspect of the celebration. Ideally, the responsibility for making the judgment lies not with the pastor, but with the pastoral planning committee. The reasons seem clear. Suitability, style and particulars are involved, and these require the judgment of many, in order to reflect the multiple interests and backgrounds in any legitimately constituted Christian community. Plurality is a constitutive element of Christianity; all people—slaves, wives, husbands, children, harlots, tax collectors, sinners, the retarded—are not only welcome, but are primary to the gospel community. Ideally, the committee represents these multiple interests more accurately than one individual. (Do we need to examine our committee make-up?)

In applying the pastoral judgment to a particular community celebration, there are four components that need to be examined:

the faith of the community, the location or space, the historical moment and finally, the culture of the community.

The faith of any community varies not only from member to member, but (as the document implies) from community to community. It is a truism to state that "on any given Sunday, within any given parish in the country," there are members of the congregation who are marginally involved in their religion (perhaps struggling with whether they believe at all), members who are deeply involved (perhaps struggling with a decision to surrender all of their earthly goods and follow the Master in a radical change of their lifestyle), and a large number of members somewhere in the middle of these two extremes. Music appropriate to all three groups must be consciously chosen.

Beyond the faith of individuals within a community, some entire communities take on characteristics which typify their faith response. However, we must caution against stereotypes. Anyone with a pastoral sense will know that "elderly" does not mean "conservative" music; black does not necessarily mean "soul" music; teenage does not necessarily mean "folk" or "guitar" music. "Old" pastors, "liberal" planners, and "hip" parents often produce these liturgies, based on the planners' needs rather than the community's needs. "People are not ready for that" reflects a feeling of the planner rather than the community. Measuring the faith commitment of a given worshiping community requires a sensitive thermometer indeed, and the temperature needs to be rechecked often.

The pastoral judgment considering place involves resources available (or lack of), people, buildings, time, money, personalities and so forth. The university parish with symphony instrumentalists in the congregation is one obvious example; the small farming community of 35 members in the congregation is another. It deals with discovering and utilizing all the talents and potentials present in the community, as well as living graciously with the specific limits of the community. It is a question of scale, of proportion, of judgment. Fr. Aidan Kavanagh's example in this matter is worth requoting: "I have seen a performance of Vivaldi's *Gloria* destroy a modest act of worship because it was far grander than, took as long to sing as the rest of the service combined...(it was) like putting the baroque dome of St. Peter's on a Dairy Queen stand" (*Pastoral Music*, 1:4). We err in this direction far too frequently. A full chorded gusto version of "A Mighty Fortress Is Our God" accompanying a solemn entrance procession consisting of two poorly clad servers accompanying a rushing celebrant down the center aisle is out of proportion. So is most of the music that is performed poorly; it is frequently more than a group, be it choir/cantor/congregation, can do well.

The judgment regarding age or the historical moment enters into the planning only occasionally; or better, once established, needs only periodic review. In terms of Church we are moving into the post-Conciliar age, and in terms of our country we are well into the last quarter of the 20th century. Our Church encourages us to "adapt," to be willing to try change (certainly in ways never dreamed of in 1950), and our country encourages us to "settle in" (certainly different from the street era of the late '60s). Musical selections reflect "our age," and are contingent on our sensitivity to the shift that is almost imperceptibly occurring in each "age."

Culture, too, enters into planning only occasionally, but seems particularly important for efforts in our time because we have had so little experience with the opportunity for integration of culture and worship due to the "liturgical freeze" following the Council of Trent. The Roman Rite we have inherited has striven to be "trans-cultural" (applicable to all nations and all groups of people simultaneously). Many theologically question a ritual that is from no culture, for no culture. Defining the American culture is not a task to be left only to the sociologists, for each of us participates in and makes up in our lives, our culture. U.S. Steel, Ford Motor Company, Pepsi Cola, Macy's, the Wild West, the Big Apple, T.V., Small Town, USA, and so on all have a bearing on our music. The language (texts) that we use, the images that we choose, the melody lines, the relation of singer to community, the role of singing in our society, all dramatically affect every liturgical celebration and song that we sing. No musical planner can ignore these elements and how they affect (or perhaps in our case fail to affect) the music chosen for the worship of God.

In a further effort to struggle with this most important but elusive judgment, the document emphasizes, as it has throughout, that worship is not a written text but a lived experience of people. "No set of rubrics or regulations of itself will ever achieve a truly pastoral celebration of the sacramental rites." Taken at face values, this is perhaps the most radical and most ignored statement of liturgical reform. The pastoral judgment presumes a sense of values on the part of the judgment maker, values that speak to scale and proportionality, values based on knowledge of the liturgy and skills of communication. The pastoral judgment presumes a deep sense of faith in the judgment maker, sensitive to the struggle of faith within each member of the community and the community at large. The pastoral judgment presumes ability to discern and make judgments, correct judgments, based on past experience and the best interest of all concerned. Pastoral judgment is no excuse maker; it demands more on the part of the musician than any other judgment.

Music in Catholic Worship: Section IV

GENERAL CONSIDERATIONS OF LITURGICAL STRUCTURE

Music in Catholic Worship: Section V

APPLICATION OF THE PRINCIPLES OF CELEBRATION TO MUSIC IN EUCHARISTIC WORSHIP

GENERAL CONSIDERATIONS OF LITURGICAL STRUCTURE

42. Those responsible for planning the music for eucharistic celebrations in accord with the three preceding judgments must have a clear understanding of the structure of the liturgy. They must be aware of what is of primary importance. They should know the nature of each of the parts of the liturgy and the relationship of each part to the overall rhythm of the liturgical action.

43. The Mass is made up of the liturgy of the word and the liturgy of the Eucharist. These two parts are so closely connected as to form one act of worship. The table of the Lord is both the table of God's Word and the table of Christ's Body, and from it the faithful are instructed and refreshed. In addition, the Mass has introductory and concluding rites.[22] The introductory and concluding rites are secondary.

The Introductory Rites

44. The parts preceding the liturgy of the word, namely, the entrance, greeting, penitential rite, Kyrie, Gloria, and opening prayer or collect, have the character of introduction and preparation. The purpose of these rites is to help the assembled people become a worshipping community and to prepare them for listening to God's Word and celebrating the Eucharist.[23] Of these parts the entrance song and the opening prayer are primary. All else is secondary.

If Mass begins with the sprinkling of the people with blessed water, the penitential rite is omitted; this may be done at all Sunday Masses.[24] Similarly, if the psalms of part of the Liturgy of the Hours precede Mass, the introductory rite is abbreviated in accord with the *General Instruction on the Liturgy of the Hours.*[25]

The Liturgy of the Word

45. Readings from scripture are the heart of the liturgy of the word. The homily, responsorial psalms, profession of faith, and general intercessions develop and complete it. In the readings, God speaks to his people and nourishes their spirit; Christ is present though his word. The homily explains the readings. The chants and the profession of faith comprise the people's acceptance of God's Word. It is of primary importance that the people hear God's message of love, digest it with the aid of psalms, silence, and the homily, and respond, involving themselves in the great covenant of love and redemption. All else is secondary.

The Preparation of the Gifts

46. The eucharistic prayer is preceded by the preparation of the gifts. The purpose of the rite is to prepare bread and wine for the sacrifice. The secondary character of the rite determines the manner of the celebration. It consists very simply of bringing the gifts to the altar, possibly accompanied by song, prayers to be said by the celebrant as he prepares the gifts, and the prayer over the gifts. Of these elements the bringing of the gifts, the placing of the gifts on the altar, and the prayer over the gifts are primary. All else is secondary.

The Eucharistic Prayer

47. The eucharistic prayer, a prayer of thanksgiving and sanctification, is the center of the entire celebration. By an introductory dialogue the priest invites the people to lift their hearts to God in praise and thanks; he unites them with himself in the prayer he addresses in their name to the Father through Jesus Christ. The meaning of the prayer is that the whole congregation joins itself to Christ in acknowledging the works of God and offering the sacrifice.[26] As a statement of the faith of the local assembly it is affirmed and ratified by all those present through acclamations of

faith: the first acclamation or Sanctus, the memorial acclamation, and the Great Amen.

The Communion Rite

48. The eating and drinking of the Body and Blood of the Lord in a paschal meal is the climax of our eucharistic celebration. It is prepared for by several rites: the Lord's Prayer with embolism and doxology, the rite of peace, breaking of bread (and commingling) during the "Lamb of God," private preparation of the priest, and showing of the eucharistic bread. The eating and drinking is accompanied by a song expressing the unity of communicants and is followed by a time of prayer after communion.[27] Those elements are primary which show forth signs that the first fruit of the Eucharist is the unity of the Body of Christ, Christians loved by Christ and loving Him through their love of one another. The principal texts to accompany or express the sacred action are the Lord's Prayer, the song during the communion procession, and the prayer after communion.

The Concluding Rite

49. The concluding rite consists of the priest's greeting and blessing, which is sometimes expanded by the prayer over the people or another solemn form, and the dismissal which sends forth each member of the congregation to do good works, praising and blessing the Lord.[28]

A recessional song is optional. The greeting, blessing, dismissal, and recessional song or instrumental music ideally form one continuous action which may culminate in the priest's personal greetings and conversations at the church door.

APPLICATION OF THE PRINCIPLES OF CELEBRATION TO MUSIC IN EUCHARISTIC WORSHIP

General Considerations

50. Many and varied musical patterns are now possible within the liturgical structure. Musicians and composers need to respond creatively and responsibly to the challenge of developing new music for today's celebrations.

51. While it is possible to make technical distinctions in the forms of Mass—all the way from the Mass in which nothing is sung to the Mass in which everything is sung—such distinctions are of little significance in themselves; almost unlimited combinations of sung and recited parts may be chosen. The important decision is whether or not this or that part may or should be sung in this particular celebration and under these specific circumstances.[29] The former distinction between the ordinary and proper parts of the Mass with regard to musical settings and distribution of roles is no longer retained. For this reason the musical settings of the past are usually not helpful models for composing truly liturgical pieces today.

52. Two patterns formerly served as the basis for creating and planning liturgy. One was "High Mass" with its five movements, sung Ordinary and fourfold sung Proper. The other was the four-hymn "Low Mass" format that grew out of the *Instruction of Sacred Music* of 1958. The four-hymn pattern developed in the context of a Latin Mass which could accommodate song in the vernacular only at certain points. It is now outdated, and the Mass has more than a

dozen parts that may be sung as well as numerous options for the celebrant. Each of these parts must be understood according to its proper nature and function.

Specific Applications

a. ACCLAMATIONS

53. The acclamations are shouts of joy which arise from the whole assembly as forceful and meaningful assents to God's Word and Action. They are important because they make some of the most significant moments of the Mass (gospel, eucharistic prayer, Lord's Prayer) stand out. It is of their nature that they be rhythmically strong, melodically appealing, and affirmative. The people should know the acclamations by heart in order to sing them spontaneously. Some variety is recommended and even imperative. The challenge to the composer and people alike is one of variety without confusion.

54. In the eucharistic celebration there are five acclamations which ought to be sung even at Masses in which little else is sung: Alleluia; "Holy, Holy, Holy Lord"; Memorial Acclamation; Great Amen; Doxology to the Lord's Prayer.

The Alleluia

55. This acclamation of paschal joy is both a reflection upon the Word of God proclaimed in the Liturgy and a preparation for the gospel. All stand to sing it. After the cantor or choir sings the alleluia(s), the people customarily repeat it. Then a single proper verse is sung by the cantor or choir, and all repeat the alleluia(s). If not sung, the alleluia should be omitted.[30] In its place a moment of silent reflection may be observed. During Lent a brief verse of acclamatory character replaces the alleluia and is sung in the same way.

"Holy, Holy, Holy Lord"

56. This is the people's acclamation of praise concluding the preface of the eucharistic prayer. We join the whole communion of saints in acclaiming the Lord. Settings which add harmony or descants on solemn feasts and occasions are appropriate, but since this chant belongs to priest and

people, the choir parts must facilitate and make effective the people's parts.

The Memorial Acclamation

57. We support one another's faith in the paschal mystery, the central mystery of our belief. This acclamation is properly a memorial of the Lord's suffering and glorification with an expression of faith in his coming. Variety in text and music is desirable.

The Great Amen

58. The worshippers assent to the eucharistic prayer and make it their own in the Great Amen. To be most affective, the Amen may be repeated or augmented. Choirs may harmonize and expand upon the people's acclamation.

Doxology to the Lord's Prayer

59. These words of praise, "For the Kingdom, the power and the glory are yours, now and forever," are fittingly sung by all, especially when the Lord's Prayer is sung. Here, too, the choir may enhance the acclamation with harmony.

b. PROCESSIONAL SONGS

60. The two processional chants—the entrance song and the communion song—are very important for creating and sustaining an awareness of community. Proper antiphons are given to be used with appropriate psalms verses. These may be replaced by the chants of the *Simple Gradual*, by other psalms and antiphons, or by other fitting songs.[31]

The Entrance Song

61. The entrance song should create an atmosphere of celebration. It helps put the assembly in proper frame of mind for listening to the Word of God. It helps people to become conscious of themselves as a worshipping community. The choice of texts for the entrance song should not conflict with these purposes. In general, during the most important seasons of the Church year—Easter, Lent, Christmas and Advent—it is preferable that most songs used at the entrance be seasonal in nature.[32]

The Communion Song

62. The communion song should foster a sense of unity. It

should be simple and not demand great effort. It gives expression to the joy of unity in the body of Christ and the fulfillment of the mystery being celebrated. Because they emphasize adoration rather than communion, most benediction hymns are not suitable. In general, during the most important seasons of the Church year—Easter, Lent, Christmas, and Advent—it is preferable that most songs used at the communion be seasonal in nature. For the remainder of the Church year, however, topical songs may be used during the communion procession, provided these texts do not conflict with the paschal character of every Sunday."[33]

c. RESPONSORIAL PSALM

63. This unique and very important song is the response to the first lesson. The new lectionary's determination to match the content of the psalms to the theme of reading is reflected in its listing of 900 refrains. The liturgy of the Word comes more fully to life if between the first two readings a cantor sings the psalm and all sing the response. Since most groups cannot learn a new response every week, seasonal refrains are offered in the lectionary itself and in the Simple Gradual. Other psalms and refrains may also be used, including psalms arranged in responsorial form, metrical and similar versions of psalms, provided they are used in accordance with the principles of the Simple Gradual and are selected in harmony with the liturgical season, feast or occasion. The choice of the texts which are not from the psalter is not extended to the chants between the readings.[34] To facilitate reflection, there may be a brief period of silence between the first reading and the responsorial psalm.

d. ORDINARY CHANTS

64. The fourth category is the ordinary chants, which now may be treated as individual choices. One or more may be sung; the others spoken. The pattern may vary according to the circumstances. These chants are the following.

Lord have mercy

65. This short litany was traditionally a prayer of praise to

the risen Christ. He has been raised and made "Lord" and we beg him to show his loving kindness. The sixfold Kyrie of the new Order of Mass may be sung in other ways, for example, as a ninefold chant.[35] It may also be incorporated in the penitential rite, with invocations addressed to Christ. When sung, the setting should be brief and simple in order not to give undue importance to the introductory rites.

Glory to God

66. This ancient hymn of praise is now given in a new poetic and singable translation. It may be introduced by celebrant, cantor, or choir. The restricted use of the Gloria, i.e., only on Sundays outside Advent and Lent and on solemnities and feasts,[36] emphasizes its special and solemn character. The new text offers many opportunities for alternation of choir and people in poetic parallelisms. The "Glory to God" also provides an opportunity for the choir to sing alone on festive occasions.

Lord's Prayer

67. This prayer begins our immediate preparation for sharing in the Paschal Banquet. The traditional text is retained and may be set to music by composers with the same freedom as other parts of the Ordinary. All settings must provide for the participation of the priest and all present.

Lamb of God

68. The Agnus Dei, is a litany-song to accompany the breaking of the bread, in preparation for communion. The invocation and response may be repeated as the action demands. The final response is always "grant us peace." Unlike the "Holy, Holy, Holy Lord," and the Lord's Prayer, the "Lamb of God" is not necessarily a song of the people. Hence it may be sung by the choir, though the people should generally make the response.

Profession of Faith

69. This is a communal profession of faith in which ". . . the people who have heard the Word of God in the lesson and in the homily may assent and respond to it, and may renew in themselves the rule of faith as they begin to celebrate the Eucharist."[37] It is usually preferable that the Creed be

spoken in declamatory fashion rather than sung.[38] If it is sung, it might more effectively take the form of a simple musical declamation rather than that of an extensive and involved musical structure.

e. SUPPLEMENTARY SONGS

70. This category includes songs for which there are no specific texts nor any requirement that there should be a spoken or sung text. Here the choir may play a fuller role, for there is no question of usurping the people's parts. This category includes the following.

The Offertory Song

71. The offertory song may accompany the procession and preparation of the gifts. It is not always necessary or desirable. Organ or instrumental music is also fitting at the time. When the song is used, it need not speak of bread and wine or of offering. The proper function of this song is to accompany and celebrate the communal aspects of the procession. The text, therefore, can be any appropriate song of praise or of rejoicing in keeping with the season. The antiphons of the Roman Gradual, not included in the new Roman Missal, may be used with psalm verses. Instrumental interludes can effectively accompany the procession of preparation of the gifts and thus keep this part of the Mass in proper perspective relative to the eucharistic prayer which follows.

The Psalm or Song after Communion

72. The singing of a psalm or hymn of praise after the distribution of communion is optional. If the organ is played or the choir sings during the distribution of communion, a congregational song may well provide a fitting expression of oneness in the Eucharistic Lord. Since no particular text is specified, there is ample room for creativity.

The Recessional Song

73. The recessional song has never been an official part of the rite; hence musicians are free to plan music which provides an appropriate closing to the liturgy. A song is one possible choice. However, if the people have sung a song after communion, it may be advisable to use only an instrumental or choir recessional.

f. LITANIES

74. Litanies are often more effective when sung. The repetition of melody and rhythm draws the people together in a strong and unified response. In addition to the "Lamb of God," already mentioned, the general intercessions (prayers of the faithful) offer an opportunity for litanical singing, as do the invocations of Christ in the penitential rite.

Progress and New Directions

75. Many new patterns and combinations of song are emerging in eucharistic celebrations. Congregations most frequently sing an entrance song, alleluia, "Holy, Holy, Holy Lord," memorial acclamation, Great Amen, and a song at communion (or a song after communion). Other parts are added in varying quantities, depending on season, degree of solemnity and musical resources. Choirs often add one or more of the following: a song before Mass, an Offertory song, the "Glory to God" on special occasions, additional communion songs or a song after communion or a recessional. They may also enhance the congregationally sung entrance song and acclamations with descants, harmony, and antiphonal arrangements. Harmony is desirable when, without confusing the people, it gives breadth and power to their voices in unison.

76. Flexibility is recognized today as an important value in liturgy. The musician with a sense of artistry and a deep knowledge of the rhythm of the liturgical action will be able to combine the many options into an effective whole. For the composer and performer alike there is an unprecedented challenge. They must enhance the liturgy with new creations of variety and richness and with those compositions from the time-honored treasury of liturgical music which can still serve today's celebrations. Like the wise householder in Matthew's Gospel, the church musician must be one "who can produce from his store both the new and the old."

77. The Church in the United States today needs the services of many qualified musicians as song leaders, organists, instrumentalists, cantors, choir directors, and composers.

We have been blessed with many generous musicians who have given years of service despite receiving only meager financial compensation. For the art to grow and face the challenges of today and tomorrow, every diocese and parish should establish policies for hiring and paying living wages to competent musicians. Full-time musicians employed by the Church ought to be on the same salary scale as teachers with similar qualifications and workloads.[39]

78. Likewise, to ensure that composers and publishers receive just compensation for their work, those engaged in parish music programs and those responsible for budgets must often be reminded that it is illegal and immoral to reproduce copyrighted texts and music by any means without written permission of the copyright owner. The fact that these duplicated materials are not for sale but for private use does not alter the legal or moral situation of copying without permission.[40]

COMMENTARY ON 42–78

Beyond Words and Concepts to the Survival of Mrs. Murphy

BY AIDAN KAVANAGH

Rev. Kavanagh, OSB, Professor of Liturgics at the Divinity School of Yale University, is a monk of St. Meinrad Archabbey, Associate Editor of Worship *and* Studia Liturgica, *and founder of the Murphy Center for Liturgical Research at the University of Notre Dame.*

Two things strike me as remarkable, among others. The first is that the Second Vatican Council began its work of Church-wide reform and renewal by addressing itself to the matter of liturgical worship. If this causes you to yawn, perhaps you either do not know, or have forgotten, how well-nigh impossible it is to get almost 3,000 Roman Catholic bishops even into the same room, much less to agree on anything—especially liturgical worship. It was even worse 15 years ago. A sizeable minority of them were against the whole idea; a small minority of them were desperately concerned that it be given priority; the majority of them were apathetic on the question. Most of them voted for the "Constitution on the Sacred Liturgy" because they perceived, as one of them said, that the front office wanted it that way—proving once again that the Holy Spirit persists in blowing in the oddest places and in the oddest ways, and that authoritarianism does have its advantages.

The second thing that strikes me as remarkable is that a three-fold revolt that began in 1832 and led inexorably to the Second Vatican Council focused on liturgical worship from its very beginning. The Oxford Movement of Keble, Pusey, and Newman had a strong liturgical emphasis from the very first—an emphasis that was easily caricatured by its opponents as mere "ritualism" and which did tend to get bogged down in romantic fascination with the middle ages and, oddly enough, in a certain obsessiveness with the worst aspects of Italian baroque. The German theological wing of the revolt quickly got into liturgical matters through its concern for the concept of the church and incarnational theology, producing an appreciation for romanesque art that was canonized in centers of German Christian culture such as Maria Laach. The French wing of the revolt, centering at Solesmes around its abbot and founder, Prosper Guéranger, took the restoration of monastic life (patterned rather on medieval Cluny) and of the liturgy itself as its main concerns.

One should not be distracted by criticisms of the revolt as being romantic. Certainly it was romantic, as Queen Victoria was Victorian and St. Augustine was Augustinian. The revolt's leaders were men of their times, and none more than Prosper Guéranger. Yet within his romantic vocabulary Guéranger was much in advance of his times. He insisted, for example, that the so-called Gregorian chant be restored in such a way that it could once again be used in parishes. While he waxed romantic over its ancient Romanness (not realizing that most of it was composed in Franco-German monasteries after the 9th century), his proposal arose from concerns that were not merely antiquarian pedantry. The chant's monodic form gave a unified musical structure to the liturgical act of the whole community met for worship, while the theatrical style of much 19th century church music reduced the congregation to liturgical passivity for lengthy periods during the act of worship. By urging participation by all in the liturgy, Guéranger sought to give everyone, not just the expert theologian or musician, a stake in the Church and its worship. He perceived the Church as a commonwealth of faith, not as a place where individuals might come merely to have sacraments and doctrine and beauty doled out to them. He was on to the true nature of symbol as something that has inevitable social consequences. He was on to the true nature of ritual as rhythmic repetition. Both symbol and ritual he knew to have everything to do with social formation, cohesion, and survival. Symbol and ritual were much too serious not to be simple, austere, and powerful. His monks would show what one form of Christian community could be, especially as they sang the liturgy in free rhythm.

I have spent this time rehearsing the historical taproot of our modern awareness of the importance of liturgical worship in Christian life because one cannot adequately discuss the role of music in worship without some idea of how much more is involved in the discussion than just how to choose an appropriate anthem. Against the background I have attempted to raise so far, allow me now to say something about how I, for one, view the function of music in liturgical worship.

First, music in liturgical worship is in a context that is far different from its place in the concert hall. Liturgical worship is a service, a ministration, to a community of faith that assembles not for a concert but for other reasons—to ritualize in symbolic activity its own deepest values, values that transcend the ordinary ones of this world, and by so doing to reinforce its own cohesion for the sake of the survival of the community in all its members. Those vital values are carried in the *life of the community itself*, not in words or books or confessional statements or libraries. Ritual-symbolic activity, which is what liturgical worship is, thus serves the life of the community assembled most immediately: ultimately that power-laden activity serves the maintenance of those values by which the community lives. Those vital values for a Christian community are summed up in the gospel of Jesus Christ, the very core of which is the paradoxical law that life comes only through death. He who would obtain life must learn how to lose it. Jesus himself was obedient to the law in the consummation of his own earthly course: his followers can do no less than remain obedient to the same law both corporately and individually. Thus Christians begin their lives of communal faith by celebrating their deaths in him at the regular table whereon lie his sacramental body broken and his blood poured out for love of all people. Their lives of prayer, fasting, asceticism, and works of mercy are extensions of baptism and the Eucharist into the needs of a world which, because it knows death only as an end to everything, finds life elusive at best, or meaningless and shot through with the nausea of hopelessness at worst. Music is a part of the service liturgical worship renders a Christian community of faith.

Second, I want to strengthen what was just said. Music is an *integral* part of liturgical service to communities of faith. Liturgically, music is not merely present in worship as Muzak is present in elevators or Mantovani's strings are present at dinner. Music is the mode, with ceremonial choreography, by which the liturgical act gets done. Liturgy is a sung act for good reasons—the same good reasons, I suspect, for which I have never heard "The Star Spangled Banner" recited. An unsung liturgy, no matter how frequent its doing, is an abnormal liturgy. People who sing at celebrations are normal, people who do not are abnormal. (The fact that a lot of liturgies and a lot of people are abnormal proves no more about my principle than the fact that many folks are neurotic proves that people in general are not human.) Liturgy is a sung act. It may be done with or without instruments, but its aural *fabric* is musical—which is to say, again, music is not merely present *in* it, but is an integral dimension of the act itself. Without music, a liturgical act loses much of the rhythmic structure that is so important in ritual activity. The ritualness of the act is itself reduced if not suppressed altogether, and as this occurs I find that the correlative visual rhythm of ceremonial choreography becomes harder to sustain. When the ritual rhythms of sound and sight disappear, what one is left with is more a seminar or a classroom lecture—modes of activity that separate more than integrate, and which make pure symbolic communication well-nigh impossible to achieve. Communities do not cohere around seminars: but everyone loves a parade. And parades are the most inauspicious acts for conducting seminars in that I know. (In this light, I must say that I suspect the "anthem view" of music in worship asumes music to be an adjunct to worship rather than an integral part of the act itself. The anthem gets added to the worship event in much the same way a coffee break is added to a seminar.)

This leads me to observe, thirdly, that what I have called the "anthem view" of music in worship may well be the presumption that has given rise to the distinction of "sacred" as distinct from "secular" music we all seem to start making when we move toward singing or playing something in church. Looking out at the matter from within liturgical tradition, so to speak, it appears to me that this distinction breaks down precisely when music as an integral part of liturgical worship is concerned. Liturgical music is neither "sacred" nor "secular": it is liturgical. Which is to say *liturgical music is any music that serves the assembled faith community and its values in ritual engagement.* Perhaps musicologists far more competent than I in such matters can tell me which and how many of the basic German chorale melodies originated as "sacred" pieces of music exclusively. The many medieval and early renaissance polyphonic Masses based on the theme of *"L'Homme armee"* derived from what was originally a secular melody sung by troubadours. And it seems that many basic melodic themes found in Gregorian chant were so popular in their origin that they were used as much in village pubs and dances as they were in church at Sunday Mass, only the texts being different. Good music is good music wherever it is found. Because of liturgical music's distinctive service to the ultimate survival of people of faith, I would advocate this be the criterion for musical selection for liturgical use rather than the criterion of whether or not a piece is "sacred." Gounod's *"Sanctus"* is patently "sacred music," but it is certainly not what a Christian people *can* sing, or deserve to have sung at them, at the Eucharist. "Good Night Sweet Jesus" and "Sweet Hour of Prayer" are even worse.

Fourth, I wish to emphasize that liturgical music, like liturgical art in general, is a constrained art form. It is constrained by the nature, purpose, and form of the faith assembly itself. The *purpose* of the assembly is worship in spirit and in truth—not education, not entertainment, not slogan rattling, not genteel cultural or moral uplift. The *nature* of the assembly is symbolic and ritual. The *form* of the assembly is communal and participatory. This last means that the assembly's act of worship is not ministerially elitist and active, or congregationally proletarian and passive. Liturgical ministers—and this includes the choir and organist and guitarist or what have you—function in service to an active, engaged congregation. The assembly is the congregation, and ministers are members of the congregated assembly too. Some Roman Catholics have developed a warped notion of this—rushing from the former extreme when the priest did everything (even down to reciting alone liturgical hymns such as "Glory to God" and "Holy, Holy, Holy," which are intrinsic parts that belong to the whole congregation) to the opposite extreme now of having everyone do everything. This is not really liturgical participation, in which each role serves the others: it is, rather, a kind of low-level egalitarianism that destroys the ritual nature of the communal act because it requires that all have their hands full of printed texts so they will know what to say together. The ritual act becomes a choral recitation of printed texts.

The point is that liturgical music cannot fulfill its true function unless it recognizes and accepts the constraints placed on it by the symbolic and ritual nature of the faith assembly and the communal and participatory form its acts take. The minister of music must be most sensitive to these constraints by choosing and executing the music *not* for his or her professional peers *nor* for some abstract aesthetic ideal, but to serve the real needs and abilities of a real assembly meeting for worship. I have seen a performance of Vivaldi's *"Gloria"* destroy a modest act of worship because it was far grander, took as long to sing as the rest of the service combined, and involved a choir and full orchestra that numbered almost as many as were in the whole congregation. While it was executed superbly, it was seriously out of scale to the total event, turning an act of worship into a virtuoso performance. Vivaldi's *"Gloria"* demands a far more substantial ritual event than the liturgical setting given it in this instance—which was like putting the baroque dome of St. Peter's on a Dairy Queen Stand.

Fifth, I wish to emphasize the importance of rhythm in liturgical worship. Some sort of rhythmic pulse is necessary to get people really together into the critical mass needed for them to become and act as one social body. The larger the group the more need for rhythm there seems to be. Seminars need little or no rhythm: football games, political conventions, parades, dances, orgies, and solemn High Mass need lots of rhythm and need it well calibrated. Drums can work Africans into a frenzy; bagpipes can cause Scotsmen to weep or kill; rocking back and forth can soothe a crying baby or push an orthodox Jew into a contemplative trance. Rhythm—oral, aural, and visual—locks people to each other and to their common values.

Rhythm, like ritual, is repetitive: the pulse goes on even though the words may change. Litanies are a liturgical art form that have been badly used recently by clergy—who often turn them into a series of short sermonettes for or against this or that—and overlooked by musicians. It is noteworthy that the two largest rites in Christianity, the Byzantine and the Roman, begin the Eucharist with solemn rhythmic litanies that were originally processional in nature—the Byzantine litany of peace (or *Irenike*), and the Roman "Lord Have Mercy" (which consists now of the congregation's responses to invocations that have since evaporated). Neither of these litanies was penitential in character, and both place less emphasis on the content of the invocations than they do on the rhythm of prayer as it alternates between deacon or cantor and the people. It seems to be a case of the sung rhythmic medium being the message rather than the content of the words. The same is true of the "Holy, Holy, Holy" and "Lamb of God," and to some extent of the "Glory to God" though not of the sung Creed. Litanies, "Holy, Holy, Holy," "Lamb of God," and "Glory to God" are popular acclamations with short responses that are easily memorized so as to free the people from printed texts. This freedom permits visual rhythm to become an effective dimension of the unifying function of liturgical ritual. (It is difficult if not impossible to choreograph a recited text of brief duration, but a rhythmically sung text such as a litany or a good metrical hymn almost demands ceremonial movement.) Composers who turn "Lamb of God," "Holy, Holy, Holy," and "Lord Have Mercy" into penitential plaints do so in the face of these chants' phenomenology.

Music in the liturgy as ministry, music as an integral part of the very fabric of worship, music in worship as liturgical rather than as "sacred" or "secular," music in worship as communally functional, and music in worship as rhythmic. These five characteristics surely do not sum up everything that can be said about the role of music in worship, but they do express the things a liturgical scholar would like to put before a group of concerned musicians and pastors.

Too long have liturgy and music been separated—largely because liturgists and musicians have gone their separate, distinctive ways. Not only has each of us suffered because of this: our respective crafts have suffered even more. What is infinitely worse, however, the communites of faith we each would serve have been stunningly pauperized by our respective monologues with ourselves. Liturgists give them texts to recite, and musicians give them concerts to listen to. Neither of our respective gifts by themselves will make them a people vibrant in the faith that may be the world's salvation.

The quiet revolts of 140 years ago have now put us all in a position where this hope may be fulfilled once again. But it will remain only a hope as long as our two professions continue to diverge. At

Yale, in the Institute of Sacred Music, we have begun to stretch toward this hope very modestly—by locking liturgists and musicians together in the same program until they learn at least to talk to each other. The first years of this have been (as one might have suspected) a rough-and-tumble time of shots from the hip, wounded feelings, some confusion, lots of frustration, some insight, two or three successes, and a lot of work. But we have begun to train some performers who can think, and some thinkers who can also perform. Those who can do neither need not apply. Who knows? In a few years of this we may even discover an answer or two that may help Mrs. Murphy survive. Then it will all have been worth it.

Making the Gathered Assembly a Worshiping Community

BY RALPH KEIFER

Dr. Keifer is a Professor of Liturgy at Catholic Theological Union, Chicago, Illinois.

The introductory rites present a challenge to the musician. This challenge draws the line between those who are merely providing some music at the beginning of Mass and those who are actually functioning as pastoral musicians by doing what worshipers need and the official liturgical norms call for.

The official norms state that the purpose of the introductory rites is to "help the assembled people become a worshiping community and to prepare them for listening to God's Word and celebrating the Eucharist." This means, in terms of the real needs of people at worship, that by the time the opening prayer has come to a close, the congregation should have a sense that they are gathered together prayerfully in the presence of God, that they are both relaxed enough and attentive enough to settle down to hear the readings with a sense of their importance and urgency, and that in some way they look forward to the celebration of the Eucharist as an action that will be fully their own. And if they are to be enabled to come to all this, the experience of the introductory rites must touch their hearts as well as their minds. The God who speaks to the Church is alive and present; he does not speak from a dead past and he is not simply a purveyor of ideas. He is also a God who calls a people together, not the devotional object of isolated individuals. Song obviously has an important role to play here: through song a congregation can share the fact that God is present among them and for them.

I describe the effort to suggest all this in song as a challenge. Neither the rites as they appear in the liturgical books nor many of the conventions of parish practice lend themselves very well to accomplishing the intent of the introductory rites or serving the needs of people "to become a worshiping community." First, the rites themselves are more complex than they should be—entrance song, greeting, penitential rite, "Lord Have Mercy," "Glory to God," opening prayer. The inevitable result of the effort to use *all* these elements at any one Mass is a disappointment. There is less a sense of gathering together in prayer in the presence of a gracious God than there is a sense of "getting through" a disparate series of devotional exercises. Say, for instance, that Mass begins with a procession and vigorous entrance song. By the time the ministers reach the sanctuary and the celebrant greets the people, there is a sense of gathering together as one people, a sense of anticipation, joy, expansiveness. If the music has gone beyond the trivial, both in its inherent quality and in its use, the celebrant will turn to face a congregation ready to pray, to listen, to celebrate. One might think that after a simple greeting, a quiet pause, and a brief prayer from the celebrant, that the congregation would be truly ready for "listening to God's Word and celebrating the Eucharist." But no, they must still get through the penitential rite and all the rest before going on to the Liturgy of the Word. Except during Lent, the penitential rite is too readily experienced as a jarring *non sequitur* to the entrance hymn. It is not at all evident why an entrance hymn that bonds a people together in praise and affirmation should be followed by a gesture of penitence, much less that it should be followed by the miniature examination of conscience that much poor practice has made out of this gesture. There is, of course, nothing wrong with beginning the Eucharist in a penitential spirit. But it makes no *emotive* sense to bob from praise to penitence back to praise in rapid order, as is required if the rite is followed literally as it stands in the book.

The juxtaposing of disparate elements in the introductory rites destroys any prospect that they can be experienced as a coherent rite of preparation leading into the readings. Frequently, too, song for the "Lord Have Mercy" and "Glory to God" is neglected. In many ways, this neglect indicates a certain sensitivity on the part of musicians. Many congregations would feel overburdened if they were expected to sing a "Lord Have Mercy" and "Glory to God" in addition to an entrance hymn. Except for special festive occasions, and with more choral support than the average parish can muster, the use of all this musical material would be more apt to weary a congregation than prepare it for celebration. The result, or course, is that "Lord Have Mercy" and "Glory to God" tend to be recited, even on festive occasions. The result of this effort to "get through" the material in the book is that by the time the readings have begun, the congregation has sung a little, recited much, and the celebrant has had a few words to say. Whether by this time they are any better prepared to hear the readings than they would have been shortly after the entrance hymn is an open question.

Conventions of parish practice in recent years create even more of a difficulty. Few celebrants seem to know how to greet the people in their own words in such a way as to lead them into prayer. Commonly, the celebrant follows the formal greeting with words to the effect that "The theme of today's liturgy is . . ." Theme worship has become something of a staple of liturgical planning and its jargon, and warrants a brief attack. The purpose of the liturgy, any liturgy, is not to promote a theme, but rather to celebrate the mystery of God with us. We are present to praise him and to be reconciled to one another; we are certainly not present primarily to imbibe some new idea, or even to reflect on old ones. To reduce the content of the prayer and readings to a slogan (theme) is to miss the point of what the liturgy is intended to communicate and evoke. The liturgy is intended to engage people (not merely minds), and a theme-oriented celebrant's introduction badly distorts the prayerful engagement that has already been set through the singing of an entrance hymn. To stand for a song and then to have the song followed by the statement of an idea is to move from an act that engages heart, body, and mind to one that engages (at best) merely the mind. If music is to be effective in the introductory rites, celebrants must learn to respect the wholeness of liturgical communication that music is. If celebrants cannot take their cue from the entrance song (by an invitation that leads to prayer, not merely thought), then silence is the better course.

Yet another convention of parish practice is the over-inflation of the penitential rite by turning the "Lord Have Mercy" into a kind of examination of conscience. The Sacramentary contains more than 20 examples of ways in which "Lord Have Mercy" may be used, and none of them approaches it in this way. The "Lord Have Mercy" is intended to be an expression of faith and trust in the merciful Christ, an acclamation of him as Lord and Savior. It cannot be felt to be such if it is interspersed with reproaches to conscience. And it is doubtful if it can be felt to be such without music that suggests Christ's tender mercy, as many of the old Latin *Kyries* did.

All things considered, it seems to be the better course to *select* certain elements of the introductory rites, depending on the season and occasion, rather than attempting to use them all at once. *Music in Catholic Worship* hints at this approach by observing, "Of these parts the entrance song and the opening prayer are primary. All else is secondary." In a similar fashion, the document urges that the musical setting of the "Lord Have Mercy" be brief and simple so as not to give undue importance to the entrance rites. Also, the document highlights the festive character of the "Glory to God." There is nothing festive about a recited "Glory to God," and it may well be asked what its recitation adds to the introductory rites. Better, perhaps, to limit use of the "Glory to God" to times when this anthem can be sung with the splendor it deserves. The same can be said of occasions when the rite of blessing and sprinkling with holy water is used. Normally, this rite will be preceded by an entrance hymn, and the rite sensibly calls for the singing of an appropriate antiphon during the sprinkling. It is anticlimactic to follow such a dramatic rite with a recited "Glory to God," and a sung "Glory to God" in this case is apt to prove to be just too much preparation. In such a case, the introductory rites verge on becoming a service of their own.

If certain elements of the introductory rites were selected each time, it would be possible to alternate and combine music, gesture, silence, and the prayer of the celebrant in such a way that the introductory rites could function as a genuine introduction. Efforts to use all the elements of the introductory rites at one time inevitably make them either too complex or too long or too confusing, or simply incoherent. Consider, for instance, the short shrift given the entrance song (two or three stanzas in most cases). It is natural enough that this should happen—with all the rest of the introductory rites to be "gotten through," the musician is hesitant to press for a longer entrance song. But the result is that the congregation is cheated of the preparation for prayer that music often provides.

This is not necessarily a call to shorten the introductory rites. The needs of congregations and the kind of celebration will make for variation in the length of time required to "help the assembly become a worshiping community." A simpler and less cluttered pattern in the introductory rites might well take longer than it does to belt out two verses of an entrance hymn and rattle along with recitation until the introduction mercifully comes to an end in the opening prayer. Keeping in mind that the entrance song and the opening prayer are the most important elements of the introductory rites, here are some possible future revisions that would result in simpler yet more appealing and effective ways to begin Mass: *simple form:* entrance hymn, celebrant's greeting, opening prayer; *penitential form (e.g., during Lent):* entrance hymn, penitential rite or "Lord Have Mercy," opening prayer; *more prolonged simple form:* entrance hymn, celebrant's greeting, sung "Lord Have Mercy," opening prayer; and *solemn festal form:* entrance hymn, celebrant's greeting, sung "Glory to God," opening prayer.

The directives of the Sacramentary itself should be taken seriously. The Sacramentary presents itself as providing norms and guidelines for liturgical celebration, not rigid rules or straitjackets.

The Sacramentary does urge judicious selection: "It is thus very important to select and arrange the forms and elements proposed by the Church, which, taking into account individual and local circumstances, will best foster active and full participation and promote the spiritual welfare of the faithful" (*General Instruction*, No. 5).

Establishing the Importance of The Word

BY PATRICK W. COLLINS

Fr. Collins is Director of the Office of Worship, Peoria, Ill., and a member of the ICEL Subcommittee on Music.

Nothing is more important for a successful celebration of the Liturgy of the Word than establishing clearly what is important and what is not. Liturgists use the word "rhythm" to describe the ebb and flow, the pace and the highlighting that must be present in an effective celebration. *Music in Catholic Worship* states clearly the order of things in the Liturgy of the Word: "The readings of scripture come first." This simply means that if any other part of the Liturgy of the Word takes on more importance—whether it be the Responsorial Psalm or the homily—then the Liturgy of the Word lacks rhythm. These priorities are set because Christ is present in the Word, truly present.

It is of primary importance that the people hear the Word of God and respond to it. Frequently, however, people fail to respond to the Word because they simply have not heard it. Delivery by lectors is often of such poor quality that congregations cannot understand what the lectors are saying. Nothing can compensate for this lack. Musicians trained in voice projection could help a parish liturgy program immensely by assisting with the training of lectors.

The proclamation of the Word is developed further by the homily, Responsorial Psalms, Profession of Faith, and General Intercessions. Homilies are generally improving. Initially, clergy thought that the homily, as compared with the sermon, was an exegesis of the scriptural text rather than a doctrinal statement. Slowly we are beginning to view exegesis of the text as a part of the "homework," and the heart of the homily as the application of the readings to the lives of the congregation present. The homily must therefore be experiential, not merely doctrinal, and the components of the homily must focus on lifting up the lives of the people. The homily not only explains the reading, it interprets the reading in the context of the lives of the people gathered. The homily breaks open the meaning of the Scriptures for the particular assembly at a particular time.

The overall criterion for judging our liturgical celebrations is rhythm or pace. The Responsorial Psalm, the Profession of Faith, and the General Intercessions, while important, are subordinate to the Proclamation of the Word. In fact, a musically developed Responsorial Psalm can easily dwarf the Scripture reading, and can certainly devastate a poorly proclaimed Scripture reading. This can be avoided only by making the musician a part of the liturgy planning team.

The first rule about the Alleluia is this: if it is not sung, it may be omitted. This cannot be emphasized enough. It is perfectly ridiculous for the reader or the celebrant to address the congregation with the spoken words: "Alleluia, alleluia, alleluia." An additional possibility is to repeat this triple Alleluia after the Gospel, especially if it is a solemn Gospel. Another conclusion to the Gospel is for the cantor or the reader, at the end of the Gospel, to sing "This is the Gospel of the Lord." The congregation then sings an appropriate response, such as "Praise to you, Lord Jesus Christ."

The Alleluia is one part of the liturgy that any congregation can and should learn to sing, omitting the verse. But even when the Alleluia and the other acclamations are the only texts used with music, it is important that they be introduced into the liturgy with an awareness of the rhythm and timing required in all liturgies. The Alleluia is an important ritual in Christian tradition. We should sing it often and well. It heightens the tone of every liturgy.

For the musician, the effective execution of the Responsorial Psalm presents perhaps the most difficult problem of all the musical texts in the liturgy. There is a theoretical problem, an execution problem, a resource problem, and a legal problem. The theoretical problem is in the nature of the Responsorial Psalm itself. Historically, the psalm following a reading served as a response. Some practitioners, however, are beginning to experience the Responsorial Psalm as a "reflection" on the Word—rather than a response—which in turn leads to response. (Psychologically—and musically—there is a difference.) We need to savor the Word of God; we need to let it sink in. To facilitate reflection, *Music in Catholic Worship* states, there may be a period of silence between the first reading and the Responsorial Psalm.

We need to clarify that the Responsorial Psalm has a dual nature, that response to the Word will come only from adequate reflection on the Word. The execution problem involves moving from silence to song. An ideal method would be for a cantor, after a period of reflective silence, to begin the first measure of the refrain in a very soft voice, building to a full voice as the congregation joins in. The response then would come forth from the reading *and* the reflection.

To use this technique with a psalm, however, requires a well-trained cantor who is immersed in the spirit and has a well-developed sense of the liturgical celebration. Without such a cantor, the response to the Scriptures can flop, miserably. It easily can become too long. It can degenerate into one set of words after another. Sadly, it often does.

The nature of the Alleluia is acclamation. Liturgists, however, cannot agree on how to define "acclamation." We have picked up a "historical" word about which we are experientially uncertain. What is really supposed to happen here? A joyful shout? A solemn proclamation? A burst of enthusiasm? A statement of faith? Perhaps all of these. But characteristically, the acclamation should be spontaneous: the text and melody so familiar that there is no need for printed material. The acclamation should explode and resound from the congregation. The acclamation need not necessarily be sung loudly or fast, or even joyfully; but it should be sung spontaneously.

The nature of the acclamation creates a dilemma for the learning of a new acclamation. How is it possible to learn both music and text of a new acclamation and to become so familiar with it that one needs to refer neither to words nor music? A learning period for an acclamation seems to deny its spontaneous nature.

The Gospel Acclamation should function as a spontaneous preparation for hearing the reading of the Gospel. It is a processional acclamation. In contrast to the Responsorial Psalm, it is related to what is to come (the Gospel) rather than what has preceded it (the first reading). The posture accompanying the Alleluia enhances its meaning. The person reading the Gospel should pace his or her arrival at the pulpit for the reading of the Gospel to coincide with the conclusion of the Gospel Acclamation and immediately be ready to say "The Lord be with you" as a continuation of the acclamation. The congregation generally should be standing during the singing of the acclamation. One procedure, developing in and among small groups, is to begin the acclamation while sitting and then rise at some point near the middle of the acclamation, thus avoiding the starkness of merely standing up and singing. In effect, the Alleluia draws you up out of your seat. Nothing violates the liturgy more than a phrase such as, "Please stand for the Alleluia."

The normal structure of this prayer is, first, an Alleluia intoned by the cantor and repeated by the congregation, then a verse sung by the cantor and an Alleluia again by the congregation. The one-line verse by the cantor can be an effective means of highlighting the theme of the Gospel because it tells what to listen for in the Gospel. However, the text of the verse is sometimes very generic; if so, it should be omitted. Too many words in our liturgies result in oversaturation of the congregation. When the Alleluia is sung without the verse, it can be enhanced by raising each Alleluia a half step and thereby building up to the Gospel. It might even be repeated three times.

Then there is the resource problem. *Music in Catholic Worship* envisions a wide selection of seasonal refrains to be sung throughout an entire season, enabling a congregation to use music repeatedly from Sunday to Sunday. This model has not developed quickly because we do not have the musical settings the Simple Gradual called for in the document. We do not have an abundance of settings for those responses, and the melodic lines of those that have been set tend to be musically poor. The result is boredom for the average congregation. Antiphonal singing will not be successful until there are antiphons sufficiently attractive to hold our attention.

Music published by Composer's Forum is a notable exception. Unfortunately, however, their antiphonal music is not very well known. The antiphons are eminently singable and easy. Sometimes the cantor's part is difficult, but seldom is this true of the antiphons. If we could get good compositions into an accessible format, we could solve some of the problems of the Responsorial Psalm.

The problem of limited repertoire of good antiphons is further compounded by the legal aspects. The specific directive in *Music in Catholic Worship* states that "the choice of texts which are not from the psalter is not extended to the chants between the readings." The important intention of this directive is to maintain a scriptural response to a scriptural reading. The Vatican Council reaffirmed that Christ is present in the Scriptures. We tend to limit his presence to the reading of the Scriptures by the lector or priest. But Christ also is present in the response of the congregation: both in their sung response and in their daily lives. We need to be reminded of this fact again and again.

The unfortunate result of the directive is that many appropriately paraphrased settings that are well done musically are categorically excluded from use. Congregational participation requires musical settings that are singable. Such compositions are unfortunately rare.

Aware of these problems, let's look beyond the present law to possible recommendations for the future. On a pastoral level, several major forms of Sunday liturgies seem to be developing: a solemn liturgy, a celebrative liturgy, and a more reserved, ordinary liturgy. For the solemn liturgy, the present practice of cantor and congregational response would remain as common practice. For the celebrative liturgy, a period of silence flowing into a single refrain repeated slowly and reflectively might be possible. Another possible model would be silence followed by a sung response, then soft instrumental music followed by the refrain. This method allows the individual to consider how the Scripture message affects one's life. It then leads to response: a single, simple response. It avoids the problem of the cantor providing additional content, and the congregation does not have to deal with complicated texts and melodies. For the more reserved ordinary liturgy, especially where a cantor is not available, silence might be the best choice. Present compromises that result in the lector reading the Responsorial Psalm immediately after the first reading are ineffectual. The practice fulfills the letter of the law, but not its purpose.

The recommendation that the Profession of Faith not be sung except on special occasions—and then sung to a simple melody—has been generally accepted throughout the United States. The words in English are simply not poetical: they are theological. And while it was possible to sing them in Latin with some sense of drama and poetry—e.g., *"et incarnatus est"*—it is not so in English. Looking beyond the existing directives, perhaps the communal statement of faith need not be required on every Sunday. It might be reserved for special occasions: the sacraments of initiation, for example, and other important faith moments.

In small group settings following the homily, a freer format might be developed using a litany form. Statements of faith could be personal and spontaneous, with the response affirmed ritually by the entire community. Major statements of personal faith could be made in a litany format, reflective of the Scripture readings and homily (e.g., "I believe that Christ Jesus is present within this community...."); these statements are affirmed by the community with an appropriate phrase (e.g., "Amen," "We believe this"). This might be concluded with the last portion of the Nicene Creed, "We believe in the forgiveness of sins...," thus relating to the universal nature of faith. This would allow the community to respond in specific terms to the Scripture readings and the homily with an affirmation of faith. This format, of course, would not be used prior to a spontaneous prayer of the faithful.

Among the several litanies of the liturgy, the Prayer of the Faithful is to gather the needs of the congregation (both individual and community) stimulated by the Gospel and homily of that particular celebration, and to unite them to the universal needs of the Church in a prayer of petition. We not only believe, we believe our God is powerful, and with us, and so we communicate to him our needs as they flow out of reflection.

The form of the prayer of the faithful is not that of an acclamation, or a response. It is a *prayer* in litany form.

Music in Catholic Worship makes the significant point for musicians that "litanies are often more effective when sung." In a genuine sung litany, the inner rhythm of the petition—the juxtaposing of petition and response—establishes the insistent pleading tone associated with the petition prayer form.

The Western Church by and large has not captured the spirit of this form at all. We have so concentrated on the content of our prayers that the form, even though critical in this case, has been ignored. Without an appropriate form, the litanies, including the Prayer of the Faithful, have languished in our celebrations. Except for the melody of the Litany of the Saints, the Western Church does not even have any music for the litany format. The Eastern Rite melodies might well be adapted for this purpose. Some of the most stimulating liturgical singing occurs in a congregation of the Eastern Church singing the response to a litany in two- or three-part harmony. We would do well to build up this tradition.

More attention needs to be given to developing the use of the sung litany throughout the entire liturgy—at the breaking of the bread, at the rite of penitence, and perhaps even during some processional moments—so that this becomes standard music in the liturgy. It would be an interesting challenge for composers to develop a litany format consistent with the three liturgical moments of the "Lamb of God," "Lord Have Mercy," and the Prayer of the Faithful.

With the emphasis on content in the Prayer of the Faithful, several styles are emerging. One is a formal series of petitions with a predetermined response (e.g., the baptismal or marriage prayer of the faithful contained in this ritual). Another is a prepared series of petitions drawn up either by the locally used parish worship aid or missalette or the local parish planners with a whole range of responses for the congregation, usually announced before the petitions. Finally, there is a spontaneous petition that is highly personalized and particular to a given celebration, with or without a response.

Those involved in developing the second and third styles would do well to examine closely the format and content of the first style. A petition in the litany must be very brief and to the point. Too often when written out, but especially when spontaneous, the petition can become a declaration of intent or an adaptation of the homily—or a counter statement to the last spontaneous petition! So many clauses, "that they may . . .," "that they may . . .," become a homily—and a poor one at that. If it is spoken it is bad, but on the rare occasions when it is sung, it is even worse. While an obvious compromise on occasions when a cantor is not present, a spoken refrain sometimes is joined to a sung response. This method is enhanced if instrumental accompaniment links the spoken word to the sung response.

When the Prayer of the Faithful is developed spontaneously, each petition should be only a brief "for our bishop" or "for the poor," and there should be no sung response.

COMMENTARY ON 47, 56–58

The Eucharistic Prayer Requires More than a Musical Flourish

BY JOHN BARRY RYAN

Dr. Ryan is Associate Director of the Murphy Center for Liturgical Research and Assistant Professor in the Theology Department, both at the University of Notre Dame.

The most serious pastoral problem posed by the Eucharistic Prayer is that it has not received the catechesis it deserves. Thus, the BCL statement takes much for granted about the Eucharistic Prayer by repeating the description given in the Sacramentary. If we review the shape of the prayer and how it functions, we shall understand the possibilities it opens up for the parish musician.

The simplest way of getting at this shape is to place it against the background of the three 1968 prayers. We praise and thank the Father by acclaiming his creation and the work of his Son, who the night before he died took bread and wine and shared them with his disciples. Gathered together, we act in remembrance of the Lord Jesus and offer the bread of salvation and life-giving cup, sanctified by the Holy Spirit. We pray for the living and the dead in union with the saints, thus cutting across space and time and the realm of the seen and unseen. We close with a formula praising God.

While it would be wrong to think that all prayers fall neatly into this flow, its outline is relatively simple:

Praise to the Father for creation
and for sending the Son Who gave his life for us
and also his Spirit in whose power we act.
Praise to the Father, Son, and Holy Spirit.

In various prayers, this outline is developed, remolded, or even commented upon.

We stand in the tradition of the disciples who took meals with Jesus throughout his life as well as in the upper room the night before he died and whose presence after his death, they experienced in the breaking of the bread.

Our Eucharistic Prayer sums up the praise all Christians give when they come together to acknowledge their victory in Christ: they belong to a world whose creation though very good had been marred by sin until transformed radically in the history of a person, Jesus of Nazareth, the Word become flesh. In this way the Eucharistic Prayer makes sense of the ritual of sharing a bit of bread and a sip of wine: taken from creation, the work of human hands is transformed.

As a prayer of thanksgiving, we acknowledge the Father's love for us; in a prayer of sanctification, the bread and wine become for us the body and blood of Christ; and we ourselves as body of Christ are nourished by this banquet of love.

Thus, the Eucharistic Prayer discloses cosmic proportions. It tells us of a hidden purpose to all life that frees us from being prisoners of our past. Moreover we look forward to sitting at table in the kingdom at the same time that we know our Eucharist leads us to build a world now where the deep-seated hungers and thirsts of all people may be satisfied.

When the BCL statement says, "The meaning of the prayer is that the whole congregation joins Christ in acknowledging the works of God and offering the sacrifice," the Roman Catholic emphasis on the sacrifical aspect of the Mass is introduced. From one point of view, the Eucharistic Prayer is itself the sacrifice of praise offered by Christians. Beyond this, in acknowledging that the once-for-all sacrifice was for us, we unite ourselves to Jesus who went voluntarily to his death. To participate in the Eucharist is to acknowledge that one intentionally aligns oneself with Jesus, crucified for us and raised up by the Father. To eat and drink with Jesus at the Eucharist is to make present the once-for-all sacrifice, thereby acknowledging the source of our faith and nourishing it at the same time.

In the face of such death-defying affirmations, what people could remain silent? The sense of people's parts in the Eucharistic Prayer is that they develop, comment upon, prolong, and ratify the words of the priest who presides at the Eucharist.

In this as in many other cases, the whole is greater than the sum of its parts. The people here and now gathered to celebrate the Eucharist are more than so many individuals (a body count, as it were). They are the local church, the concrete manifestation of the Catholic Church. They are at this moment in time the Church. The rite to which they belong protects them from being thrown back upon their own very real limitations.

With a variety of Eucharistic Prayers in English, we are now in a better position to see the function of the people's vocal parts. These parts make sense only if the entire Eucharistic Prayer is seen as the prayer of the entire people of God. Fittingly enough one person plays a central role in expressing the prayer, but from the very outset it is clear that it is the prayer of each and every one of the assembled. First of all, the presiding priest may briefly introduce the Eucharistic Prayer by suggesting reasons for giving thanks that are appropriate to the particular group of people gathered together. The familiar dialogue that opens the prayer functions as an invitation to a prayer that belongs to all the people: Let us give thanks to the Lord our God.

Experimental Eucharistic Prayers have been composed that are meant to be entirely sung by presiding priest, choir, and congregation. In the Roman Rite we do not yet have such Eucharistic Prayers whose very texts are influenced by their being created for musical composition. For this reason, in our present prayers, our sung parts sometimes come across as mere accessories, pretty flourishes as it were or extended musical pieces to be listened to—or interruptions in the flow of the prayer.

Just as the Eucharistic Prayer recited by the presiding priest or concelebrants is of one piece and belongs to him and the people, so too do the people's parts: the "Holy, Holy, Holy," the Memorial Acclamation, and the Amen. The relationship is a dialogic one. The way the presiding priest leads into these parts has a great influence on the way people participate in the liturgy. The organ accompaniment is meant to add volume to the human voice, but too often the people experience their timid voices being drowned out by it. When this happens we end up back where we started from, wondering how to get the people to understand the Eucharistic Prayer as their own and their part in it vital to the total effect.

Right after the acknowledgement of God's greatness in the Preface (which is supposed to have a certain hymnic quality), the presiding celebrant and the people join their acknowledgement of praise and glory to that of the heavenly hosts. The "Holy, Holy, Holy" in the very shape and choice of its words shows the influence of ancient Asian languages. This has helped keep it as a traditional set piece. Its function is to join the voice of the people to that of the presiding priest as they now unite their earthly liturgy to the eternal heavenly liturgy. Since the "Holy, Holy, Holy" is part of a larger prayer which had its own internal unity long before it made room for the set piece, composers should keep it in moderate bounds when setting it to music. This means the parish musician has to make a judgment with regard to its sung length. Its development should not be so long that it takes on a greater importance than it has in the total prayer. Choirs that sing a complicated "Holy, Holy, Holy" run the risk of taking to themselves a part that legitimately belongs to all the people, thereby leaving both presiding priest and people marking time. Each of the eight new Eucharistic Prayers (the three 1968 ones, the three for children, and the two for reconciliation) takes up some expression from the "Holy, Holy, Holy" to continue its prayer so that the set piece is integrated into the total prayer.

The Memorial Acclamations differ from the "Holy, Holy, Holy" in several ways; for example, the flow of the prayer is deliberately interrupted and the people acknowledge the living presence of Jesus. Whatever words are used, they are meant to be a victorious acclamation of faith. In capsule form they give the sense of the Eucharist: a memorial of a living person: the risen, glorified Jesus, who suffered and died for us.

These acclamations, with the exception of the first, are addressed to Jesus. It is a way of acknowledging and making sense of the presence of Jesus in the community as we remember his redemptive death inseparably linked to his resurrection, ascension, and coming again.

The children's Eucharistic Prayers are one place where legitimate experimentation with the acclamation is possible. These prayers, now in the third year of their three-year trial period, allow for other acclamations than those prescribed. This is true of the memorial acclamations as well as other acclamations used throughout certain sections of the prayer. Here too an effort must be made to relate the acclamations integrally to the prayer.

There is no liturgical reason why additional acclamations cannot be used in the 1968 prayers. In fact, the statement seems to encourage it when it calls variety in the acclamation desirable. In the past several years, the BCL has commissioned several eucharistic prayers with additional acclamations, so a much needed expansion has begun.

The Amen at the end of the Eucharistic Prayer is called the Great Amen because of the importance of the prayer that is being ratified. Perhaps its very brevity has led people to join in the final "Through Him, with Him, in Him" trinitarian praise formula called the doxology. It is desirable that this Amen not fall flat, but it inevitably does so wherever it is taken for granted. In many parishes when the concluding doxology is not sung, the Great Amen comes across as a muffled congregational hiccough. It would seem that only when the Amen is sung could it be saved from falling into oblivion. Often it gets lost. But the Our Father comes to its rescue to get us all out of an embarrassing situation. How different was the Amen for Ezra's people:

Ezra blessed the Lord, the Great God and all the
people, their hands raised high, answered,

"Amen, Amen!" Then they bowed down and
prostrated themselves before the Lord, their
faces to the ground.

But that was in another time and another culture when bodily
gestures were more naturally integrated into prayer. In comparison with this, our Amen is a pitiful remnant. It cries out for
repetition and development.

What can be done? The people's parts in the Eucharistic Prayer
can be given priority in the pastoral situation. If there is going to
be any singing at the Sunday Mass, then it ought to be the people's
parts in the Eucharistic Prayer that are sung; if anyone is going to
be employed to help the people sing, the priority should go to
leading the people in singing and not simply accompanying them
on the organ. The presiding priest and the parish musician can
learn the function of the Eucharistic Prayer and how the people's
parts belong to the whole prayer. They can learn that the "Holy,
Holy, Holy," Memorial Acclamation, and Amen function differently. Thus, they can plan to favor their functioning as part of
the total context of the Eucharistic Prayer. In a well sung
Eucharistic Prayer, presiding priest and parish musician have to
work together learning how to lead in and out of the people's
parts. Also since the shortest Eucharistic Prayer (II) does not need
a developed Amen as much as the longest prayer (IV) does, the
musician should know ahead of time which prayer is going to be
used. When the people's parts do not function properly, we find
that the prayer tends to become the presiding priest's own, the people feel incidental to the whole rite, spectator participation takes
over, and the presiding priest becomes an object getting through
his thing. Against these and other difficulties our liturgical
renewal continues to struggle.

COMMENTARY ON 48, 59, 62, 67–68, 72

Word, Song and Gesture Articulate the Communion Rite

BY FREDERICK R. McMANUS

Father McManus is Vice Provost of the Catholic University of America, Washington, DC. and serves on the Board of Directors of the Center for Pastoral Liturgy at Catholic University.

The greatest contribution of the 1972 recommendations entitled *Music in Catholic Worship* is that they place music in context and in proportion. When we look at the music of a clearly distinct part of the eucharistic celebration such as the Communion Rite, all the valuable specifics of *Music in Catholic Worship* are enhanced by the proportion the document gives among the particular elements of the rite and complemented by the context of the musical, li-turgical and pastoral considerations in which the music of wor-ship should be composed, selected, and carried out. The whole document should be read and reread as a whole by musicians and pastors alike.

To be specific, however, the Communion Rite first may be characterized as a part, area, or zone of the eucharistic liturgy with several significant components. These components articulate the common Christian meal (itself an act rather than words or song): the Lord's Prayer; the Sign of Peace; the Breaking of Bread; the Communion; [the period of silence and/or song]; and the prayer after Communion.

Looking at it schematically, the musician (and, it is hoped, the pastor and other priests and indeed all who prepare for a worthy and effective celebration) will immediately attach the elements of song to these five parts:

1. The Lord's Prayer (sung by priest and people);
2. The Sign of Peace (without song);
3. The Breaking of the Bread (accompanied by the singing of the *Agnus Dei*);
4. The Communion (accompanied by the communion song); [The Period of Silence and/or Song];
5. The Prayer after Communion (recited or chanted by the priest).

Each element will receive its comment below, but the primary point is not the sequence of individual parts. The primary point is not even the relative significance of the texts ("The principal texts . . . are the Lord's Prayer, the song during the communion procession, and the prayer after communion.") It is rather that the words, song and gestures articulate the holy action, which is the eucharistic meal of God's people. Or, to go deeper into the meaning of that eucharistic meal, as the 1972 document expresses it well, "Those elements [of the common rite] are primary which show forth signs that the first fruit of the Eucharist is the unity of the Body of Christ, Christians loving Christ through loving one another.

All this is needed to put into context, and to suggest the proportions of, the distinct elements of the Communion Rite that may be clothed with song.

The Lord's Prayer has been called the table prayer of the eucharistic banquet. It is the prayer we say before we sit down (figuratively on most occasions) as the "table companions of God." Before the Second Vatican Council, the longstanding tradition of the Roman Liturgy had been for the presiding priest to sing it (or recite it) alone. True, the priest began by inviting the congregation to pray with him (silently), and there was a concluding response by the people who sang (or said) the last clause. But it was clearly a "priest's part" of the celebration.

The reform of the Roman liturgy deliberately assigned the singing of the Lord's Prayer to the people, together with the priest. As much as any other part of the Mass, it is a communal affirmation of faith. In itself, it is surely the most important element of the Communion Rite to be sung.

Music in Catholic Worship notes that the Lord's Prayer "may be set to music by composers with the same freedom as other parts of the Ordinary," but "settings must provide for the participation of the priest and all present." Even as recently as ten years ago, it may not have seemed likely that the Lord's Prayer would be sung regularly by congregations. Experience has now demonstrated, both from the popularity of a couple of contemporary settings and from the widespread familiarity of one or two chant melodies, that we can expect the Lord's Prayer to be sung almost as easily and as simply as the Holy, Holy, Holy or Alleluia.

Music in Catholic Worship properly mentions that the doxology, although it is separated by the saying or singing of the embolism ("Deliver us, Lord, from every evil . . ."), should also be sung. In fact the integral character of the Lord's Prayer as the first element and most important text of the Communion Rite will be lost otherwise. Another note worth adding is that, while various settings and harmonizations of the Lord's Prayer are available, it is very important that nothing—instrumental accompaniment, choral parts, or other—make it difficult for this principal Christian prayer to be sung by all together: priest and ministers, people and choir.

Before the reform the Sign of Peace (called more often the *pax*, or kiss of peace) was a lengthy rite. It was conceived as the peace extended from the altar (the symbol of Christ) to the presiding priest and then in turn from him to the deacon, the other ministers, clergy, servers, singers, and (rarely) through the congregation (by the kissing of an image or pax-brede).

In practice this complex and lengthy rite was seen only at pontifical and solemn Masses; it followed the breaking of the consecrated bread and appeared to be a kind of exceptional prelude to Communion for the clergy.

The reform changed all this. The Sign of Peace is now a simple and distinct rite, a suitable sign or gesture (handclasp, handshake, embrace, whatever is usual in each locale) exchanged with those nearby. It is no longer thought of as a sign transmitted from the priest to the deacon to the servers and so on. Rather each one exchanges the greeting before Communion with his or her neighbors in the assembly. Thus it can be a distinct and joyous element of preparation for Communion, a sign of the Christian fraternity gathered at the Lord's table. (Pastoral specialists and liturgical purists might prefer that it take place earlier in the Mass, before the gifts are placed on the altar, but this is another issue). It has become a universal sign that is readily recognized throughout the world, no matter what the differences in language may be. It is a small gesture to show that we are a Christian community, no matter how unknown we are to each other.

Because it is so brief, the Sign of Peace has no appointed music to accompany it. If anything is sung during the exchange of the Sign of Peace, it should be extremely brief. It should not confuse this part of the rite with the next, which is the still more significant Breaking of the Bread.

The Breaking of Bread intentionally is not entitled *Angus Dei*, although this is the litany-song that properly accompanies the breaking of the consecrated bread in preparation for its distribution to the people. As a song, the Lamb of God is quite secondary. It should enhance or support the action of the breaking of the bread for Communion, an action mentioned in every biblical account of the Lord's Supper and preserved in every Christian liturgical tradition.

Music in Catholic Worship describes the accompanying Lamb of God very simply and adequately, noting the technical point that the invocations may be repeated over and over as long as needed, with the petition; "grant us Peace," always in last place. It also notes that, since the Lamb of God is not necessarily a song of the people like the Holy or Lord's Prayer, "it may be sung by the choir, though the people should generally make the response."

Ideally the litany form of the *Agnus Dei* should be respected, with a cantor or small group singing the invocation ("Lamb of God: you take away the sins of the world" and the people, together with the choir, making each response. But other arrangements are possible; strengthening or elaborating the melody by part singing, even singing the text as a kind of motet rather than a litany. In some countries alternative texts are used, including the alternative translation composed by the ecumenical International Consultation on English Texts ("Jesus, Lamb of God:/Have mercy on us./Jesus, bearer of our sins:/Have mercy on us./Jesus, redeemer of the world:/Give us your peace."). Alternatives have not been formally sanctioned for the United States.

The weakness in this part of the Communion Rite is not in the musical settings, but in a failure of the reform of ritual. We have been so preoccupied with other issues connected with the Communion ritual (Communion received in a standing posture, Communion from the cup, Communion in the hand) that the Breaking of the Bread has been neglected. This rite signifies with greatest clarity that Christians are made one body by sharing in the one loaf. Therefore, the priest who presides should always break enough of the consecrated bread to show, in imitation of the Lord himself, that there is this common sharing in the meal.

This point is made very well in a document even more basic than *Music in Catholic Worship*, the *General Instruction of the Roman Missal*: "The eucharistic bread . . . should be made in such a way that the priest can break it and distribute the parts to at least some of the faithful" (No. 283). The usual practice is treated as second best, permissible but never to the exclusion of the ritual breaking of a generous quantity of the consecrated bread: "When the number of communicants is large or other pastoral needs require it, small hosts may be used. The gesture of the breaking of bread, as the Eucharist was called in apostolic times, will more clearly show the Eucharist as a sign of unity and clarity, since the one bread is being distributed among the members of one family" (No. 283).

The musician who works in isolation is at a loss. The reform must begin with the ritual action. Once this takes on meaning and a few moments are spent in the solemn breaking of the bread, the sung Lamb of God, whatever its style or melody, will fit properly into place as an accompaniment.

The actual Communion ritual has its accompaniment, which is the principal "procession song" of the entire Eucharist. Sometimes, through a misconception, the Communion Song has been postponed until after the Communion. It is clearly the song to unify the communicants as they come to receive the sacrament of unity.

In treating the communion song, *Music in Catholic Worship* simply quotes verbatim the formal decision of the National Conference of Catholic Bishops approving alternative texts which might replace the communion song (psalm with antiphon) designated for each Mass.

First consideration should be given, of course, to the Communion psalm and antiphon appointed in the missal—especially since a great treasury of suitable antiphons has now been added in the revised rite. But then the positive criteria are given for the substitutions: "the communion should foster a sense of unity . . . be simple and not demand great effort . . . (giving) expression to the joy of unity in the body of Christ and the fulfillment of the mystery being celebrated . . . be seasonal in nature . . . (or) topical, provided these texts do not conflict with the paschal character of every Sunday." The negative side is just as significant: The time of sharing in the holy meal is no time for hymns or songs of adoration of the Lord Jesus. Because they emphasize adoration rather than communion, most benediction hymns are not suitable.

This is not an idle warning. One reason why congregational singing during Communion has been difficult to introduce in some places is an almost complete misunderstanding of the communal or horizontal dimension of the Eucharist as the sacrament of the Church. People who had been instructed carefully that the Eucharist was exclusively (or almost exclusively) a matter of individual personal piety were quite reasonable when they objected to the distraction of singing during the Communion procession. This objection, however, was all the more reason to encourage the Communion song—preferably in simplest style, such as responsorial—so that the misconception gradually could be erased.

Because of the diverse possibilities of the Communion song (psalm with repeated antiphon, other kinds of responsorial song, hymns, which may be alternated with choral song or instrumental music), coupled with the length of the Communion procession, it offers a rewarding challenge to musicians and priests. More than any other element of the Communion rite, the actual sharing in the banquet calls for common and joyful singing. If nothing else is sung, this should be—always keeping in mind the tone and theme of the appropriate texts, as explained in *Music in Catholic Worship.*"

In the listing above, the "period of silence and/or song" has been bracketed to indicate that it is an option. This is not to minimize its significance, but to make sure that it does not overshadow, especially in musical treatment, the Communion act itself and the Communion song which accompanies Communion. If a choice is made, the Communion song is always to be preferred to the "Lamb of God" and the song after Communion.

The present option in the Roman liturgy dates to a strong emphasis in the 1963 *Constitution on the Liturgy* on sacred or religious silence as a part of rites—a creative and dynamic silence formally introduced into the rite. The current practice also goes back to a tentative Roman recommendation in 1967 that there might be a period of silence or a psalm or song of praise of God during this period—until the whole Communion Rite is concluded with the prayer after Communion. The period can best be characterized as one of "silence and/or song of praise" because the best use of it would be for a considerable time of silence followed by the psalm or song in praise of God.

Music in Catholic Worship deals with this optional singing of a psalm or hymn of praise very simply, recommending "a congregational song which may well provide a fitting expression of oneness in the eucharistic Lord."

The 1967 Roman instruction on the subject suggested the kind of song that is appropriate: psalm 34 or psalm 150, an Old Testament canticle like the *Benedicite* (Daniel 3:57–88, 56, or Daniel 3:52–57. Another suggestion is found in the use of the canticle of Zechariah *(Benedictus)* or the canticle of Mary *(Magnificat)*, which are sung at this point when morning prayer or evening prayer, respectively, are sung at the beginning of Mass.

The period after Communion is emphatically not the time for a second Liturgy of the Word. The addition of readings, however appropriate otherwise, can distort the rite. Similarly, it is not a period of "thanksgiving after Communion" or an opportunity to add new prayer texts to the Mass ritual, again no matter how well intentioned. Above all, a certain proportion should be kept. If the Communion rite has been lengthy and has already included song and silence, anything additional may be duplicative and wearying. On the other hand, this is a very suitable period of the eucharistic rite for a complete pause for silent reflection—possibly accompanied by instrumental music and followed by a distinct congregational song of praise in hymn or psalm form.

The final element of the rite is not a song, but prayer (the "prayer after Communion") led by the priest who presides. Of course he may sing it to the recitative chant, and people and choir should always respond with the amen of affirmation. Some of the prayers appointed in the sacramentary, especially those which look from the eucharistic celebration to its effects in Christian life and living, may suggest suitable themes for the Communion song and for the (optional) song of praise after Communion.

MUSIC IN SACRAMENTAL CELEBRATIONS

MUSIC IN SACRAMENTAL CELEBRATIONS

79. While music has traditionally been part of the celebration of weddings, funerals, and confirmation, the communal celebration of baptism, anointing, and penance has only recently been restored. The renewed rituals, following the *Constituion on the Sacred Liturgy,* provide for and encourage communal celebrations, which, according to the capabilities of the congregation, should involve song.[41]

80. The rite of baptism is best begun by an entrance song;[42] the liturgy of the word is enhanced by a sung psalm and/or alleluia. Where the processions to and from the place of the liturgy of the word and the baptistry take some time, they should be accompanied by music. Above all, the acclamations—the affirmation of faith by the people, the acclamation immediately after the baptism, and the acclamation upon completion of the rite—should be sung by the whole congregation.

81. Whenever rites like the anointing of the sick or the sacrament of penance are celebrated communally, music is important. The general structure is introductory rite, liturgy of the word, sacrament and dismissal. The introductory rite and liturgy of the word follow the pattern of the Mass. At the time of the sacrament an acclamation or song by all the people is desirable.

82. Confirmation and marriage are most often celebrated within a Mass. The norms given above pertain. Great care should be taken, especially at marriages, that all the people are involved at the important moments of the celebration,

that the same general principles of planning worship and judging music are employed as at other liturgies, and, above all, that the liturgy is a prayer for all present, not a theatrical production.

83. Music becomes particularly important in the new burial rites. Without it the themes of hope and resurrection are very difficult to express. The entrance song, the acclamations, and the song of farewell or commendation are of primary importance for the whole congregation. The choral and instrumental music should fit the paschal mystery theme.

COMMENTARY ON 79

The Key to Sacraments: The Community

BY ANDREW D. CIFERNI

Rev. Andrew Ciferni, o. praem., is liturgy director at Dayles-
ford Abbey in Paoli, Pa.

At some time in the last 15 years virtually every person involved
in liturgical planning has had some experience in which the planning for a sacrament tended toward an event that would appear to
be more the elevation of an individual than the celebration of a
community. Rites of religious profession, weddings and ordinations often come across as being for the sole benefit of those entering into the sacrament. It seems that the music is chosen from the
top ten liturgical or non-liturgical "hits" of the novice, couple or
ordinand.

Seminarians who have regularly absented themselves from the
celebration of the Liturgy of the Hours are suddenly, as the time
for ordination approaches, incredibly interested in the cut of albs,
the color and placement of candles, the coordination of flowers,
the artistic merit of liturgy programs and the quality of the contra-
Bourdon stop of the cathedral organ. Rarely do we encounter the
novice, prospective bride and groom or ordinand whose first concern is the liturgical experience of the community coming together
to celebrate sacramental acts that are as much the possession of
those invited as those who sent the invitations.

Paragraph 79 of *Music in Catholic Worship* begins in mid-
stream. It affirms the musical component of weddings, funerals,
confirmations, baptism, anointing of the sick and reconciliation. It

encourages the provision for congregational song in all of these sacramental celebrations, not just the Eucharist. Before we read this *MCW* directive, we should reread the opening theological section of the document, "The Theology of Celebration," as a foundation for all of the section "Music in Sacramental Celebrations." More important, for anyone coming to the planning of a sacramental celebration, is to reread the section "Pastoral Planning for Celebration" and "The Place of Music in the Celebration."

Because both "General Consideration of Liturgical Structure" and "Application of the Principles of Celebration to Music in Eucharistic Worship" are concerned with the Eucharist and because the section on sacramental celebrations is such a summary statement, one could have the impression that questions of planning and musical evaluation apply to the celebration of the Sunday parish Eucharist alone. One indeed has this impression from current practice.

Most parish liturgy planners would not countenance on Sunday morning the sort of things that are performed and heard at Saturday's weddings. Most religious communities would not dare take as a serious part of their daily liturgical diet the sweet and fatty selections that are interjected into celebrations of religious profession. The bombast that marks many ordinations undoubtedly speaks more about the persistence of clericalism than it does about the local church's recognition of God's gifts of ministry bestowed on certain individuals in the community's midst. This is symptomatic. Many parish liturgy planners, religious and diocesan liturgy commissions still take a hands-off policy when it comes to planning special sacramental rites such as weddings, religious professions and ordinations. This reluctance exposes our deepest misunderstanding of the nature of sacramental celebrations.

What many sacramental celebrations seem to proclaim is that they are celebrations of an individual's achievement. The individual or couple on whom the celebration centers is deemed to have the right to make virtually all decisions concerning the selection of texts, music, ministers and environment because this is "his," "her" or "their" sacrament. This individual has undergone the rigors of the novitiate or the seminary and therefore has gained the right to celebrate, having run the gauntlet and survived. This becomes then an opportunity to make any number of peripheral statements. For example, I can indicate my closer friends by asking them to be ministers, regardless of the fact that they may not be suited for the ministry they are asked to perform. I can choose readings and music that clearly state my thinking about this sacrament. I can create the mood that communicates my feeling about this day.

What sacramental celebrations should be proclaiming is that they are communal acknowledgements that God has again acted in the life of the community in and through specific individuals whose status and work in the community has been changed as a result of God's freely given gift. Sacraments are not achievement celebrations. At least, they do not celebrate the achievements of the individual or the community. What they *do* celebrate are the achievements of God, who has willed to save us as a people. What God has done in the lives of individuals has been done for the sake of all. The community that gathers for a wedding, an ordination or a rite of religious profession does not come together simply to facilitate the reception festivities. Even less does the community come together to be moved by the touching sight of one of its members entering into a new public relationship to God through the Church. The community comes together for its own life—for its own act of confession.

Perhaps our reading of the MCW directive would be best preceded by a reflective reading of the second chapter of *Environment and Art in Catholic Worship.* Our past has apparently taught us that we have much to learn about the sacraments as communal celebration. Paragraph 28 speaks clearly to the matter: "Among the symbols with which the liturgy deals, none is more important than this assembly of believers." By now we have had enough experience that we can no longer show any naivete. The liturgy alone is not going to produce an authentic symbol out of this assembly of believers. As long as failing marriages are not made whole, as long as clerics are allowed to act as though they operate in splendid isolation from the communities they serve, and as long as religious pray and live as though they participate in a special variety of Christianity, then the assembly of believers will continue to regard weddings, ordinations and acts of religious profession as the private property of those being married, ordained, or professed. As long as this continues, the sacraments will not achieve their full potential as the primary expressions of the community's life, and the community will be frustrated in its attempt to realize itself as the Body of Christ.

This malaise could be addressed by a new edition of MCW. Every official pronouncement on the Church's liturgy could well begin by stressing that sacraments do not have a life independent from the daily sacrament of the community's shared experience in Christ. A Christian community in which the important decisions are made by the clerical establishment will infallibly celebrate liturgies in ways that do not take the congregation seriously. Second, a new edition of MCW could well reemphasize the need for planning and evaluation for all sacramental celebrations. Third, any new edition of MCW or any of the present sacramental rituals must attempt to give a deeper understanding of the liturgical structure of all the sacraments. Fundamental catechesis must take place or we will continue to be misinformed and malformed by the sacramental celebrations that give witness to a lot of bright ideas but little sound liturgical judgment.

Until this happens, we will continue to witness wives vesting their newly ordained deacon-husbands and parents doing the same for their newly ordained prebyter-son because no one has understood that structurally the vesting is a sign of acceptance into an *ordo*, and that those who are already members of that *ordo* are the only significant givers of the *ordo*'s vesture. Until there is a common understanding of the structure of the rite for a wedding, the community will have to bear endless moments of boredom while it stands listening to the couple's favorite song from their first date. Until religious communities have a clear vision of religious profession as a eucharistic act, we will be assailed by vow formulas that sound like valentine messages from the young religious to God.

Ultimately, these issues will be decided on the battleground of our present discussion on initiation. Initiation, of its essence, is about entrance into a community. A community that truly takes possession of its initiatory process will not surrender its possession of all the sacramental moments that flow from the logic of initiation. A community that has nurtured individuals through the trauma of a new vision of reality (what we call conversion) will not allow these individuals to simply slide into marriage by rites that are planned in total isolation from the community's sensitivities and capabilities. After an authentic initiatory experience, this would be unthinkable for the community and for the initiated individuals entering into marriage. Religious communities that have seriously faced the contemporary crisis of formation are less and less apt to allow the novice to begin planning a rite of religious profession without ascertaining that the novice has truly plumbed the community's traditions. In fact, these communities tend more and more to place the responsibility for the celebration of religious profession in the hands of the community's liturgy planners. We even see growing evidence that ordinations are being planned more and more by diocesan liturgical commissions and that they are being planned as true diocesan celebrations. This should be the inevitable conclusion of a long period of preparation (initiation) for a ministry that is one of self-emptying rather than self-aggrandizement.

Contemporary sacramental theologians are wont to say that there is either one sacrament, the Church, or an indefinite number of sacraments, the ensemble of self-expressive acts of the Church's life. The truth of either or both of these positions demands a consistent vision of sacramental activity. If initiation is necessarily a communal act, then all the acts that flow from initiation are necessarily communal. If initiation entails communal involvement and assent, then all the sacraments entail communal involvement and assent. If the culminating act of initation, the Eucharist, must be planned by the community on the basis of a deep structural understanding of the rite, then all the community's sacramental celebrations must be executed on the basis of similar planning, grounded in a similar understanding of structures. Commitments to the study and the investment of resources that this demands will be made only because the assembly of believers has found in its day-to-day life an experience of God in Christ that makes it impossible for any member to contemplate a sacramental celebration that would not take most seriously the state and condition of this Church, at this time, in this place.

Baptism
"Unless a Man Be Born Again. . ."

BY RON LEWINSKI

Rev. Ron Lewinski is Associate Pastor at St. Marcelline Parish in Schaumburg, Ill. and, as a staff member of Chicago's Office for Divine Worship, serves as editor for the Chicago Catechumenate.

At the time *Music in Catholic Worship* was being written, the Rite of Christian Initiation of Adults had not yet been promulgated in English, and so the final draft of paragraph 80 reflects the authors' dependence on its companion, the Rite of Baptism for Children. Since the publication of MCW, however, the Rite of Christian Initiation of Adults has become of increasing importance and influence in the celebration of the sacraments of initiation. The U.S. Catholic Conference of Bishops has gone as far as to say: "The primary model of Christian Initiation is the initiation of adults" (*Christian Commitment*, NCCB, 1978). This of course has led to many questions of musical interest and a desire to expand the scope of MCW's paragraph 80.

Before we discuss the musical implication of the Rite of Christian Initiation of Adults, a few comments on music for the Rite of Baptism for Children are in order. Paragraphs 79 and 80 of MCW state very simply that communal celebrations of baptism should include music, and suggestions for its appropriate use are offered. Even though the suggestions are simple enough for general use, many communities still celebrate the rite without any music whatsoever. The frequent complaint is that it is impossible to get people to sing. Some planners express discouragement when too many families seeking baptism for their children are themselves unpracticing and consequently uncomfortable with the idea of active participation, not to mention singing music they've never heard. Still others find it awkward to use music when there is only a small family group huddled around the font on a Sunday afternoon. These situations are cause for real pastoral concern, but they are not without remedy.

Many of these frustrations with music could be eliminated if baptism were celebrated more frequently in the midst of the regularly worshiping community. Ordinarily this means that baptism should take place at a regularly scheduled Sunday Mass or a specially scheduled Sunday Eucharist (monthly, bimonthly or seasonally) that the faithful would be encouraged to attend. Music at these celebrations should have a festal character and be well planned. One should never get the impression that the music is an addendum or filler in the liturgy. Even when baptisms are celebrated outside the Mass, there is still a need for music and a leader of song, who would assist the families in their responses. It is also helpful to have at least one adult who can assist at the liturgy by directing the parents and godparents to their places.

Inasmuch as the rite of infant baptism requires some form of parental preparation prior to the celebration of the sacrament, music for the liturgy could be introduced as part of the preparation. At the very least, an acclamation could be easily learned and then used in the liturgy.

The objection can be heard that the congregation doesn't want to participate in the celebration of baptism. But there is a need for us to begin instructing the faithful in their responsibility to welcome new Christians. What it is that makes sacramental celebrations *communal* is that people come together out of concern for their brothers and sisters who are to be initiated, reconciled, anointed, married or ordained. The unsuccessful use of music at baptism is frequently due to a poorly planned communal celebration of the sacrament. Even though we now have new rites for the sacraments, they are often celebrated as if nothing had ever changed. Introducing new liturgical texts and moving the font from the back of the church to the sanctuary will not automatically guarantee the liturgical spirit that is called for in the revised rites. If we continue to celebrate new rites with old attitudes, the role of music envisioned in *MCW* will never be fully realized.

The Rite of Christian Initiation of Adults has become the model for Christian initiation, for it best demonstrates the gradual conversion process that must always be part of an individual's becoming a Christian and a member of the Church. It is not simply a manual for celebrating the sacraments of baptism/confirmation/Eucharist, but a comprehensive design that may be spread over a number of years. Progressive stages of religious development are celebrated in rites and prayers that are formative as well as expressive of the candidates' spiritual progress. More than anything else, the rite stands as a firm witness to the Church's belief that Christians are made and not born. Baptism/confirmation/Eucharist are the culmination of the initiation experience, not isolated, independent rituals that automatically create mature Christians.

Furthermore, the initiation process, referred to as the "catechumenate," takes place within the community. This means that there is more to a candidate's preparation than the good efforts of the clergy. The new rite envisions that a number of the laity will be involved in the formation of a new Catholic Christian. The preparation process will include opportunities for communal prayer that certainly should include music.

Had the Rite of Christian Initiaion of Adults been available when *MCW* was written, there surely would have been some directives for making music an integral part of the preparation process leading to the sacraments of initiation. Music should accompany the rites of the catechumenate and liturgies of the Word in which candidates participate. Music used at these times does more than enhance the liturgy. Music used in the process of initiation assumes a formative role. Candidates can be formed by the music they hear and sing; melody, tonal character and text convey meaning that catechesis, homily or dialog cannot. For this reason, music for the catechumenate should be selected with great care.

What is the doctrinal content of the hymn? What kind of spirituality is conveyed? Does the music meet the mood or feeling the candidates have about their faith? These are but a few of the questions that planners should consider.

One of the richest sources for sung music suitable for catechumens is Scripture, especially the psalms. During a candidate's formation, the Word of God is the principal focus and fount of spiritual life. Candidates can easily identify with such psalms as 22, 26, 28 and 113, and these psalms can in turn be used as a basis for catechesis. Since liturgies of the Word will be *the* style of worship for catechumens, psalms can be learned and used repeatedly at those services. Other Old Testament or New Testament canticles such as Phil. 2:6–11 would also be appropriate. Sister Suzanne Toolan's *Beatitudes,* found in G.I.A.'s Congregation and Cantor series, is a very good composition to use in the formation of catechumens.

Just as music is important prior to the celebration of baptism/confirmation/Eucharist, so it is in the postbaptismal period (mystagogia), which continues the formation of new Christians. During this time, the newly initiated reflect on the sacramental mysteries that they have personally celebrated, and it is hoped that their spirituality would deepen with the privilege of sharing in the Eucharist. Music could be drawn from the lectionary as well as the sacramentary. The gospel acclamations for the Sundays of

145

Easter, for instance, are simple yet powerful Acclamations such as "I am the good shepherd. I know mine and mine know me" (4th Sunday of Easter), or "I will not leave you orphans. I will come back to you and your hearts shall rejoice" (7th Sunday of Easter) are fine examples of text that might be put to music during this period. Other postbaptismal hymns from the Scriptures that could be valuable are Eph. 1:3-10 and Col. 1:12-20, to name only a few. The Magnificat and Benedictus in the new *Lutheran Book of Worship* are also worth considering.

But what about music for the celebration of the initiation sacraments themselves? First, it should be assumed that the celebration of the sacraments of initiation will take place in the midst of the community, ordinarily at the Easter Vigil. Music should be chosen with the congregation in mind. One of the most practical considerations is the use of acclamations. Even the memorial acclamations found in the Eucharistic Prayer would be appropriate. But the rites for baptism provide a fine selection of acclamations and New Testament hymns and songs from ancient liturgies (*Rite of Baptism for Children* #225-238; *Rite of Christian Initiation of Adults* #390), which are all very useful at the celebration of sacraments of initiation. Congregations should learn a few of these acclamations or brief songs and be able to sing them from memory, recognizing them as their traditional initiation music. The celebrant or leader of song can use them whenever a brief acclamation is called for, and the congregation can respond without being tied to a printed text. ICEL has issued *Music for the Rites: Baptism-Eucharist-Ordinations.* This is a valuable source for music and should be considered.

All of the recommendations in the *MCW* directive are applicable to the rite of initiation. Although it is not mentioned in the paragraph, a very suitable moment for music in the rite of baptism is at the blessing of water. Chants for the water blessing can highlight the wonderful plan of God to use simple elements of creation for touching the lives of his people. Another choice opportunity for music in the rite is the Our Father, easily sung to the same melody used at Mass.

The recommendations for music during the procession to and from the font, when this will "take some time," should not be interpreted too rigidly as to mean *only* when this will "take some time." For even if there is a short distance to and from the font, this movement in the liturgy does signal a change of internal liturgical direction and is usually a very good opportunity for music, if only an acclamation or litany. An illustration of this is when confirmation immediately follows baptism. If the baptism has taken place in the rear of the church or in a location where the congregation could not witness the action, it would be best to celebrate the confirmation in another location where it can be witnessed by the congregation. The procession to a new location, even if it is a short distance, calls for some musical expression, perhaps a litany of praise if not a hymn.

The rite of confirmation itself is so brief that it needs to be embellished; preferably not by additional spoken words but by music. After the celebrant introduces the rite of confirmation and invites the congregation to pray for the candidates, who are asked to kneel, a meditative anthem sung by the choir (e.g., "Bless the Lord, O My Soul" by M. Ippalitov-Ivanov) can be quite effective. Music played at this point gives the assembly time to absorb the mystery of baptism just celebrated and to prepare for confirmation when the newly baptized or newly received will be sealed with the gift of the Holy Spirit.

Music is integral to the very action and meaning of liturgy; it can convey a spiritual vitality and message that spoken words cannot. It should never be used as something to break up the liturgy or dress up our responses.

It is hoped that in the future, composers will be encouraged to create new musical compositions that will enable us to see and appreciate the depth of beauty in the initiation rites. An example of future development would be to offer a musical rendition to the postbaptism ceremonies of anointing with chrism and enrobing and giving of lighted candle. These ritual gestures ought to speak for themselves with possibly some music to highlight the action rather than explain it. Thus it might be sufficient to sing "God is Light: in Him there is no darkness," rather than to speak the address attached to the giving of a lighted candle in both infant and adult baptism rites.

The challenge of the MCW directive on baptism, then, is addressed not only to pastoral planners but to church musicians and composers, who should be encouraged to create new ways to use music at the celebration of baptism and in the stages of preparation.

Anointing of the Sick
God Gives His People Strength

BY MARGUERITE STREIFEL

Sr. Marguerite Streifel is Executive Secretary for the Liturgy Commission of the Diocese of Crookston, Minnesota.

The Rite of Anointing and Pastoral Care of the Sick is one of the most far-reaching of the reforms of Vatican II. It is the sacrament that most touches the faith community at its heart, in its pain as a journeying people seeking wholeness of body and spirit. This sacrament is a means for the Church to express concern for its sick members through pastoral activity, sacramental praise and thanksgiving, and to provide a visible and tangible presence. This sacrament and the Rite of Christian Initiation of Adults may be the two strongest reminders and calls to the People of God to activate their baptismal commitment to others—to be a people warmly caring for and welcoming its members.

Since the official effective date of January 1, 1974, the Rite of Anointing and Pastoral Care of the Sick has affected the lives of countless millions. It has motivated strong efforts at catechesis and pastoral concern, and people seem to be very much aware of the rite, as they frequently receive it.

It has been five years since this revised rite was initiated. Perhaps it is time for us to examine where we have come from and where we might go with it in the future. When the revised rite for anointing became effective, *Music in Catholic Worship* was already two years old, so its compilers were unaware of the rite as it finally appeared. As we examine how this rite is being pastorally celebrated, we will look at the directions of the official ritual for the "grass roots" and at MCW to determine how it might be more specific or helpful in giving us guidelines.

A recent survey of the Diocese of Crookston, Minnesota shows 83 percent of the respondents with the correct understanding that this is a sacrament for anointing the sick. 51% of these same respondents indicated that some pastoral care is being exercised by the laity: communion is being taken to the sick or shut-ins by relatives, friends, appointed lay distributors or visitors. People are asking to be anointed before surgery or hospitalization, and these anointings are happening at daily eucharistic celebrations with other members of the faith community. In one parish in particular, 25 people take communion to the hospitals and prepare the sick for the sacrament of anointing. Lay people visit, pray with, and communicate with the sick or shut-ins on behalf of the parish community.

Communal celebrations of this sacrament are happening in 66% of the parishes. Another 15 percent believe in communal celebrations but do not yet have communal anointing. 70% have anointings communally within the context of a eucharistic celebration. The 15% who have not experienced a communal celebration indicated that they would have the anointing at a eucharistic celebration. These are encouraging figures, for they indicate· that the implications of the revised rites are gradually seeping into the consciousness of our people. We are all familiar with the truism that as people celebrate, they not only express who they are, but at the same time, *become* who they are. Our people are celebrating communally in the context of the Eucharist, the greater sacrament of healing, reconciliation, and salvation. They are taking more seriously their mutual witness of concern, care and healing.

The revised rite of anointing expresses pastoral care in two actions: in visiting and giving communion to the sick, and in the anointing of the sick. The rite for visiting and giving communion to the sick has the following elements: sprinkling with holy water, the spirit of penance, reading of the Word, the Our Father, communion, and concluding prayers. The rite of anointing presumes preparation on the part of the priest and the sick person or persons. The rite includes sprinkling with holy water, to remind us of our basic starting point; a penitential rite, to remind us of Christ's merciful, healing kindness; a reading from Scripture, a litany, the laying on of hands, the blessing of oil (or a prayer of thanksgiving over previously blessed oil), the anointing of the forehead and hands, a prayer for the sick, the Our Father, communion and the concluding blessing.

The ordinary rite of anointing is the first one given in Chapter II of the document (ICEL *Provisional Text*, The Liturgical Press, 1974). This section outlines the structure of the rite as being patterned after the liturgy of the word with the laying on of hands, blessing of oil and anointing. In reality, the rite of anointing during Mass is the most frequent practice and the focus of this article. Obviously, the order of statement in the ritual does not reflect the order of preference in practice!

Before communal anointings began in the parish of Sacred Heart in East Grand Forks, Minnesota, much groundwork was done by members of our liturgy team and by our parish Life and Action committee. To introduce the rite five years ago, we used homilies as well as films or slides and bulletin inserts. Parishioners were contacted personally by members of our core team who explained the rite and its value. This same core group contacted other parishioners to bring the elderly and the sick to the church. Students from the high school helped. Entertainment was provided at a luncheon following each celebration. (We later found that the elderly do not care to be entertained, but rather cherish this occasion as a time to visit each other.)

The liturgy was planned for an afternoon anointing on the feast of All Saints. The whole parish was invited to gather and pray with those being anointed. The choir helped with the music. We started with a moving experience five years ago and have continued every year.

In planning the liturgical celebration for a communal anointing, we are careful to include a gathering hymn, alleluia, Holy, memorial acclamation and Amen in which all can participate, in accordance with the rite: "The full participation of those present should be encouraged by the use of appropriate songs to foster common prayer and manifest the Easter joy proper to this sacrament" (#85).

During the laying on of hands, the priest is instructed to impose hands in silence. However, if there is a large number to be anointed, a musical selection is sung or an instrumental number might be done after the first few persons have received the imposition of hands. The nature of this music is quiet, such as a reflective prayer-song or an instrumental composition.

During the actual anointing, the words spoken by the priest should be audible. But here again, when there are large numbers present, we begin singing after the first few have been anointed.

There are many selections of music that are appropriate at these two moments. "Be Not Afraid," "You Are Near," and "Lay Your Hands" from NALR, "God Gives His People Strength" from Medical Missionaries; or "Come, Lord, Bring to Us Your Peace," "We Carry in Our Body," and "My Prayers Come Before You Like Incense" from St. Meinrad's are just a few examples. Psalms 22, 23, 25, 41, 63, 84, 103, 133, 139 and others from any number of sources are also appropriate. If we do our homework, we can find all kinds of musical possibilities. As for the type or the style of music used, our people do not seem to mind the style or the idiom as long as it is "prayer-song" that has something significant to say or to pray—in short, simple, provocative prayer!

In the survey conducted in the Diocese of Crookston, several observations surfaced, which are listed here.

The imposition of hands on each person and the anointing of each person seem extended when there are large numbers to receive the sacrament. However, the laying on of hands is one of the central elements in the rite of anointing and is so powerful a sign that some parishes are combining the imposition by the priest-celebrant with "touch" signs from other members of the faith community present and near the persons being anointed. One parish has a general imposition in global by the priest with a friend or family member imposing hands individually on each sick person (when large numbers are being anointed). There are some pastors who combine the imposition of hands and the anointing as one moment, instead of individual imposition, prayer for blessing the oil, and the anointing. If this manner of administering the sacrament is used, it is presumed that the oil is blessed before the two actions are performed. In any case, this element cannot be omitted or glossed over, because the rite itself is primarily, as Godfrey Diekmann asserts:

> ...a rite of touch. It demands physical closeness and communication in the deepest sense. On the part of the minister, it implies nurturing care, gentleness, affection, protection, communication of strength. On the part of the receiver, it implies openness, acceptance, confidence, a feeling of belonging, of strengthening, of well-being. To allow another person to touch you in any way is an act of openness and acceptance—in this case to the action of the Spirit. Thus the gesture is admirably suited to express and actualize the coming and presence of the Holy Spirit. The Church is a community which "touches" others.—The Laying on of Hands: The Basic Sacramental Rite," in: *Proceedings of the Catholic Theological Society of America,* 1974, pp. 350–351.

The majority of pastors prefer to bless oil at each anointing celebration because of the powerful prayer that accompanies this blessing and explicates the rite. The prayer given as the first option for the blessing of oil, however, is a rather poor choice because it is chauvinistic. A more satisfactory prayer is #242, which is also in the form of a berakah. It is unfortunate that it was not put as the first choice.

A number of parishes give a sign of life to each person anointed, such as a plant or flowers, or a candle during the Advent season. This added gesture of caring means much to those anointed. Another interesting suggestion is to have the person anointed rub the oil where the pain or sickness is located.

There are many other possibilities for innovation with this sacrament. Pastoral sensitivity and creativity are necessary on the part of pastors, parish teams, the parish council, and the liturgy committee. Whatever is planned for the sick should highlight the continuing responsibility of the local community for an ongoing, flexible pastoral service for the sick and the elderly.

A revision of *Music in Catholic Worship* would better serve our needs as pastoral musicians if a stronger statement were made, which would outline the actual rite of anointing as it is celebrated in the context of Eucharist. If we follow the good principles already laid down for good eucharistic celebrations and clarify the options of the anointing rite itself, we would have a better guide. Because pastoral practice is indicating that communal anointing should take place in eucharistic celebrations, recognition of this should be included in *Music for Catholic Worship.*

Penance
Reconciliation with Your Neighbor, Too

BY DEBORAH MUNCH

Mrs. Deborah Munch is former Director of the Department of Liturgy for the Diocese of Memphis.

Diocesan directors of music are probably familiar with the scene of the frantic liturgy team member pouring out a thousand questions about his/her recently assigned task of selecting music for an upcoming communal penance service. Because these liturgies are becoming more and more popular, and because the unfortunate criterion for assigning them to an individual music planner is often that this person has never done one before, the scene continues to repeat itself. Complicating the whole situation is the fact that *Music in Catholic Worship* (the "bible" of parish musicians) says very little about these celebrations, and that the Church has renewed its approach (thank heavens!) to the theology of sin and reconciliation. This is an attempt to answer some common questions and to order these questions into a practical process, which may simplify the challenge of the healing ministry to which the musician/liturgist has been called.

Because the *Revised Rite of Penance* was published over a year after *MCW* it is understandable that the music document gives only very general treatment of communal celebrations of the sacrament. What direction *does* the document offer? It stresses the importance of music in these celebrations; it gives a structural overview of the order of service (introduction, word, sacrament and dismissal); and it provides for an "acclamation or song by all the people" during the sacrament. For musicians and liturgists who are planning parish celebrations of Form II* (the more commonly used of the communal rituals), more specific information is available in *Study Text IV* (U.S. Catholic Conference, 1975) and the *Study of The Rite of Penance* (USCC 1975). The latter text is especially helpful because it offers model penitential liturgies, which can be used alone or adapted to include Forms II or III.* Of these examples, three are for general use, and there is one each for Advent, Lent, children, youth and the sick. Both books give a detailed order of service with accompanying rubrics and suggested texts for readings, prayers, songs, acclamations and responses. Their combined cost is approximately $7.00, and since most worshiping communities will need them year after year, the books are a must for any parish liturgical library. Of course, the celebrant will want a more attractive, more expensive large-type hardbound copy of the rite for use on the altar; this edition can double as his reference copy.

Those who are selecting music for the first time for a parish communal sacramental reconciliation liturgy and those who seldom plan them (e.g., once or twice a year), would probably find that the most practical approach doesn't begin immediately with filling in the blanks of a liturgy outline. Certainly one might want to read through the order of service, but to save backtracking and to avoid duplicating effort, the efficient musician/liturgist will begin with three preliminary considerations: the liturgical season, the sacrament and the scripture chosen for the particular celebration. The season is listed first not because it is the primary consideration (the sacrament is), but because it contextualizes the other two.

Of the three reference works listed above, only *Study Text IV* specifically mentions the liturgical season. Unfortunately, one statement makes seasonal considerations appear optional: "As with all good celebrations, the gathering begins with a song which expresses the penitential stance of the assembly or the character of the liturgical season in which the sacrament is being celebrated" (p. 33). However, an earlier section, "The Time of Celebration," reinforces the importance of season themes, as does a similar section in the study edition (#13). In the sample penitential celebrations (pp. 81–91) of the study edition, the Advent and Lenten examples clearly echo the messages of the respective seasons (e.g., the desert experience is linked with the strengthening of baptismal grace for Lent, and the second coming of Christ is linked with the

---

*Form II is reconciliation of several penitents with individual confession and absolution.

*Form III is reconciliation of several penitents with general confession and absolution.

Baptist's warning "Prepare ye the way" for Advent). These "themes" are especially important for the musician, as they affect the choice of an opening song. Ideally, they will resound in the rest of the service music as well.

Too often those who are constantly involved in the liturgical year take for granted their congregation's appreciation of the seasonal context within which the whole Church prays. Music for a Lenten reconciliation service should not only focus on reconciliation, but it should also illuminate for the congregation how reconciliation relates to some major Lenten message (conversion, transfiguration, renewal, dying to self, putting on Christ). However, this is not to say that the music should assume the role of a teaching aid; in any liturgy, music's primary role is celebrational, not educational—a point sometimes overlooked by those who plan communal penance services for children.

Apart from being thoroughly familiar with the liturgical season, the conscientious music planner should also do some reading about the sacrament of reconciliation, particularly about the historical precedents for its communal celebration, and about the nature of sin itself. *Study Text IV* offers some thoughts about the latter and suggests a bibliography. For those who are unfamiliar or uncomfortable with the community's role in Form II celebrations, the historical/theological reading will inspire enthusiasm for the communal dimension that the congregation's song will nurture, and firm up the basis on which musical judgments will depend.

A good scripture commentary is useful for a better understanding of selected reading(s). Any good homilist usually owns one or knows where to borrow one. Popular commentaries are *The Jerome Biblical Commentary* (Prentice-Hall) and *A New Catholic Commentary on Holy Scripture* (Nelson). Because of their organization, commentaries on the Lectionary are not as useful for this purpose as commentaries on the Bible. If it is not possible to get hold of a scripture commentary, the music planner should at least read the chapter from which the selected reading is excerpted. Sometimes introductions to the various books of the Bible are helpful.

Although this sounds like homily preparation, the musician/liturgist need not go into the depth that is required for a homilist. What has taken paragraphs to describe really amounts to a few minutes of reading. These few extra minutes will save time in the long run, as the prepared music planner will find it much easier to select appropriate texts.

All of the preliminary work to understand the sacrament, the season and the Scripture will be a waste of time if, in the end, the music planner surrenders to familiar, unspecific repertoire for the sole sake of its familiarity. The often-repeated excuse, "My congregation just doesn't know any appropriate hymns" reflects two

problems: the music program for building congregational repertoire is not adequate; and the musician/liturgist has too limited a
concept of "song." A song need not be one of the old-warhorse-
type hymns. There is a wealth of short responsorial refrains,
which, though possibly unfamiliar, a congregation can easily perform with the assistance of a good cantor. Another solution to the
repertoire problem is to match a familiar hymn with an appropriate text of similar meter. The metrical index in any good
hymnal is a good resource for this approach. Interchanging texts
should be handled with care, however, as some hymn tunes are
written in such a way that few texts except the original are compatible with the tune. And, of course, it is important to check
every syllable of every verse to see that nothing is out of place.
Otherwise, the results could be disastrous!

After completing the preliminary reading, which should clear
up some general questions, the musician/liturgist is ready to deal
with practical and specific questions. If the upcoming communal
reconciliation service is a first for the community or for the music
planner, there are probably many. When in the liturgy should the
congregation sing? How much solo music is needed, desirable or
permissible? How celebrational should the service music be? How
penitential?

The faithful gather as individuals who have somehow become
alienated from one another, from the Church, from God, but who
recognize the healing power of the Church through its ministers.
The very presence of the people attests to some understanding of
and faith in God's mercy and love. They do not gather in despair
of their wretched sinfulness, but as heirs to the kingdom. For this
reason, music that serves as a prelude to the liturgy should be re-
pentent, but not morbid, and should reflect a certain amount of
confidence. Somber organ variations on "Were You There When
They Crucified My Lord?" would be an inappropriate introduction
to a Lenten communal reconciliation liturgy.

So what *would* work? Of the organ repertoire not associated
with any text, Preludes Nos. 3 (E minor) and 5 (G minor) of the J.S.
Bach "Eight Little Preludes and Fugues," and Flor Peeters "Aria"
and the Alain "Dorian Choral" are examples. Because the Bach
works are standard repertoire for most organ students, citing them
as typical examples will help the organist understand what is
needed. To the organist who knows and owns more repertoire, the
music planner could suggest a chorale prelude based on a standard German chorale whose text is compatible with the particular
liturgy (e.g., "Jesus Christ, Thy Sure Defense" or "If Thou But Suf-
fer God to Guide Thee"). This is not meant to be a "grocery list"
approach to suggested organ music, but rather a practical approach to facilitating communication between organist and music
planner.

It is regrettable that *MCW* says so little about vocal or instrumental preserve music for reconciliation or any other worship services. This is, perhaps, something to consider for a supplementary publication.

If the liturgical season has indeed been considered in the overall planning (selection of readings, etc.), the individual whose only responsibilities are music planning and performance should have no difficulty understanding what type of text is needed. Sample entrance antiphons in the rite speak of God's mercy, compassion and love, and of our confident prayer for grace and strength (#48). A communal penance liturgy scheduled in the last weeks of Ordinary Time or during Advent, and in which there is an eschatological emphasis, might well begin with Lucien Deiss' "My Soul Is Longing for Your Peace." Choosing a song such as this one, reflective in character, allows for growth toward the most festive moment of the service, the proclamation of praise after individual confession and absolution. A more festive opening song might prevent this desirable contrast.

Choosing responses to readings and Gospel acclamations is a familiar task to most Catholic church musicians. When in doubt about the text of an appropriate response, the muscan/liturgist can always check the appendix of the Lectionary to see if the reading in question has been used in the Mass. If so, the response listed in the Lectionary may offer a clue. Topical indexes to the Bible are also helpful.

The music planner should be sure that the performing musicians clearly understand the number of readings and the order of service within the Liturgy of the Word. More often than not, liturgists opt for fewer than three readings in consideration of the service's overall length and the expected number of individual confessions. Musicians accustomed to performing on Sundays will need to be told that the Gospel acclamation immediately follows the response, or that preceding the Gospel acclamation there will be no other reading.

The mood and text of music for the liturgy of the word will depend to some extent on the readings to which they relate. But, as in the case of the opening song, the most celebrational music is best chosen for the acclamation of praise after individual absolution. In order for the music of the liturgy of the word to reflect a growth pattern proper to the rite, the Gospel acclamation should not be one of the most festive. "Ye Sons and Daughters" is an example of the type of song that will probably work best. Of course, if the communal penance service is held during Lent, there will be no problem.

After the homily and before the acclamation of praise, the rubrics in the order of service do not specifically mention music. It seems logical, however, that the Examination of Conscience, particularly if performed as a litany, and the intercessory litany within the reconciliation rite may be sung by all; "Litanies are often more effective when sung" (MCW #74). There should be no problem with assigning the Examination of Conscience to a cantor or choir, for the rite provides that a priest, deacon or *other minister* may assist the faithful in their examination of conscience (#53).

As the music planner considers the service as a whole, the option of silence during the examination may be a welcome relief from what might become verbal overkill in the early part of the liturgy. Choosing a spoken text, a sung text or no text for the examination is a liturgical judgment, which will depend on the extent of the local community's enthusiasm for singing and the amount of singing planned for the rest of the liturgy.

Again, the rite of reconciliation doesn't mention the use of music during individual confession and absolution. It would seem that carefully chosen solo music (rather than liturgical "muzak") interspersed, perhaps with appropriate readings and periods of meditation could add meaning to what might be a deadly lull. Because so many people will be moving in different directions at this time, congregational singing is likely to be limited.

So much has been said about the proclamation of praise after absolution that little needs to be added. Ideally, the song will praise God for his mercy and goodness and incorporate any predominating emphasis in the liturgy as a whole (e.g., darkness to light, baptismal commitment, love, etc.). This is not the time to fall into the trap of "general," unspecific texts, unless there isn't any other option. This *is* the time to drag out a parish "warhorse," something that everyone will enthusiastically sing. Beethoven's "Hymn to Joy" (van Dyke text) could work well in liturgies that emphasize love or the darkness-to-light theme. A familiar or simple responsorial setting of Psalm 98 might be a good choice in an Advent reconciliation service.

After the proclamation of praise, there need be no more music. The service ends with a closing prayer and dismissal. Some parish liturgists choose this simple ending, some add the Sign of Peace, others add a closing song and/or a postlude. Texts for closing music should express gratitude and praise with, perhaps, some mention of the Christian commitment that has been reaffirmed. Certainly, this music should be positive and can be festive; just how festive will depend on the liturgical season and the shape of the liturgical plan. Some penance services demand a denouement effect, an easing of the emotional high by lengthening the liturgy's ending. A brief ending can be an abrupt letdown. On the other hand, sometimes the less said, the better. Common sense will dictate the best course.

It is hoped that the lengthiness of this discussion hasn't obscured the real thrill of putting together rubrics, sacraments, theology, the liturgical calendar, reconversion, music repertoire and all of the accompanying considerations and molding them into a living experience in prayer. Because the sacrament of penance is a relatively infrequent experience and because the faithful are not obliged to participate, communal celebrations of the sacrament offer a rare respite from the routine. The faithful are particularly *ready* to pray and to listen as a community. The communal dimension that music reinforces in any liturgy can be especially effective in the context of a sacrament that specifically involves community building and communication. It's worth the effort.

COMMENTARY ON 82

Confirmation and Marriage
"What If . . . ?"

BY RICHARD FRAGOMENI

Rev. Richard Fragomeni is the Diocesan Coordinator of Liturgy for the Diocese of Albany.

What if the three little pigs had all built their houses out of straw? What if the Grinch had stolen Christmas for keeps? Or, what if Pope John Paul I had lived? What if the Roman Catholic Church would ordain women? What if Vatican II never happened? What if we keep asking "what if"?

"What if" is the magic phrase that opens the road to speculation and creativity. "What if" takes what is and creates from it what could be more. "What if" can unleash the intuitive mind of the human being to new horizons and interests. This form of questioning may be the key to the successful cultural adaptation and development of liturgical practice.

In applying the "what if" method to paragraph 82 of *Music in Catholic Worship*, two questions emerge: "What if we were to implement the directive as it is presently stated?" and, "What if the directive were to be rewritten—what would the new draft include?" In considering these two "what if" questions, the concern is to imagine the possible directions that their implications can give to the liturgical and musical life of the Church.

If we read the directive in the context of the rest of the section "Music in Sacramental Celebrations," this paragraph (and indeed the entire section) seems to be the unedited product of a committee process; in comparison to the conciseness of the rest of the document, this section seems to ramble. Confirmation is mentioned as if in passing, which may be understood in view of the fact that in 1972, when *MCW* was published, the rite of confirmation was still a provisional text. The problem at the time concerned the form of confirmation and the determination of the validity of the form as either a gift of God or a gift of the Father.

Confirmation as an initiation sacrament is often misunderstood. In the *MCW* directive, no provisions are made for specific incorporation of music into the confirmation rite. Rather, the directive presupposes that it is desirable that both confirmation and marriage celebrations take place in the context of the Mass. Thus, music for the Mass, to which *MCW* is primarily addressed, is also music for the confirmation and marriage rites.

The rather strong and apparently misplaced directive "that the liturgy is a prayer for all present, not a theatrical production" indicates again an editorial oversight. It's a wonder that such a statement should follow the powerful assertions at the beginning of the document: "Faith grows when it is well expressed in celebration. Good celebrations foster and nourish faith. Poor celebrations weaken and destroy faith." (*MCW* #6) The implication in #82 seems to be that the theatrical elements of celebration would weaken and destroy faith rather than build it up.

Let us apply the "what if" approach to this idea: What if we removed from our celebrations all that is theatrical? In applying the question specifically to the marriage rite, a lot would disappear: the costumes—the wedding dress, the vestments of the presiding priest or deacon, the tuxedos—all would go; the cast—the attendants, especially the flower girls and page boys—would be missing; and the setting—the parades, the music, the flowers—all that might be considered theatrical would be eliminated. What's left? The minimum: the bride, the groom, the clergy and two witnesses. (Imagine Altman's new film "A Wedding" with such a minimum of excitement, not to mention Cana of Galilee!)

Liturgical renewal has stressed from the beginning that the minimalistic approach so characteristic of the pre-Vatican II Church be replaced by a sensitive look at symbols in order to restore them to their fullness. When symbols are restored to their fullness, we see God—or *theos*, in the very derivation of the word theatrical. It is possible to involve the whole congregation in prayer and still be involved in the beauty of that which is theatrical. (For further reading, see Matthew Fox, *On Becoming a Musical Mystical Bear: Spirituality American Style*, Paulist Press, 1972.)

The Christian community, by celebrating with faith, deepens its faith. And these celebrations must be engaging and beautiful. Therefore, while we must avoid all that is self-centered, we need to recognize all that we are as individuals, all that we are able to perform and all that might be performed for God as prayer.

The directive does not say much about music, except that we are to follow the guidelines for Mass when celebrating marriage and confirmation rites. What if, however, confirmation and marriage were to be celebrated outside of Mass?

Liturgical renewal was envisioned as a two-pronged adventure: first, the rites were to be revised; and second, the rites were to be adapted culturally to the needs of churches at the local parish level. The revision of the rites has been completed; now they must be adapted.

It is in this perspective of cultural adaptation that the second question, "What if the directive were rewritten?," should be raised. It might read as follows:

> Confirmation and marriage are both personal and communal celebrations. Careful attention, then, must be given to the structure of these sacramental rites so that both dimensions are expressed. Although the Mass holds the place of prominence in the Christian community, every effort should be made to develop the rites in and of themselves with appropriate music and activity. In any circumstance, however, these rites should speak to the human person, using all the modes of the culture to do so.

Such a revamping raises the question of the relationship between the celebration of the Eucharist and the celebration of confirmation. For confirmation celebrated with children (separate from the baptismal rite) and for marriage celebrated without the Eucharist, what if the rites were developed and music were composed specifically for them? Marriage and confirmation might become rich spiritual, emotional and human experiences tailored to the needs and wants of individual communities, persons and couples. Liturgists, musicians, catechists and priests would all be involved together in the preparation for these sacraments.

Clearly, the second "what if" is open-ended. Some will say that it opens the door to endless innovation. Well, what if it did? Such speculation is necessary for the further development of liturgical practice. It is a very useful tool by which liturgy committees can educate themselves, and it can be a great deal of fun, too.

We could continue to ask "what if," not only with this directive, but with the entire document. What if we were to realize in so doing that liturgy is much more theatrical and musical and creative than we ever dreamed?

COMMENTARY ON 83

Burial Rites
"And I Will Raise
Him Up..."

BY RICHARD RUTHERFORD

*Rev. Richard Rutherford, CSC is the Chairman of the Depart-
ment of Theology at the University of Portland in Oregon, a
member and consultant of the archdiocesan Liturgy Commission
and the author of a book on the Rite of Funerals.*

Reviewing *Music in Catholic Worship* again after several years
is a fascinating and renewing experience. To do so with the liturgy
of the Rite of Funerals uppermost in mind reveals again the quality of the document as a whole. Its principles and recommendations serve the funeral as well as all other Catholic worship. It is
not a handbook, however, and one does not expect to find in it the
"how-to" answers to all the musical questions pertaining to Catholic funeral liturgy or—far less—detailed answers all wrapped up
in paragraph 83 on the importance of music in the new burial
rites. Rather, according to the principle of "The Liturgical Judgment" (#30), it is the nature of funeral liturgy itself that will help
determine what is the most appropriate pastoral music for the Catholic funeral.

In the ten years since its publication, how does this document
itself hold up today? How well are its principles and recommendations followed in pastoral practice concerning funeral liturgy? As
the contemporary saying goes, there is some "good news" and
some "bad news."

To begin with the latter question and the "bad news," few
would disagree that the American funeral remains musically the
most difficult area of Catholic worship. Pastoral publications continue to point up the many obvious reasons for this; diocesan

handbooks continue to offer suggestions to remedy the situation. However, among the principles set out in MCW and highlighted in #83, some are enjoying relative success. One is the use of *acclamations* in the funeral liturgy. To a lesser degree, the *entrance song* seems to serve well its liturgical function of creating a sense of Christian community gathered around the deceased, especially where it encompasses the American rites at the entrance to the Church. All too frequently, however, this opening song of the community is replaced by instrumental music.

Overlooked but worthy of mention in the MCW directive should be the special place of *psalms* in funeral liturgy. Like the acclamations and the entrance song, psalm responses are becoming more expressive of community at the funeral. More important, however, this use of the psalms is special because, of all our funeral chants, they remain the inspired prayer-in-song of God's people. The psalms, in ecclesial and christological faith, have served in the liturgy of funerals from its inception to express paschal hope. Their presence throughout the funeral as a whole expresses in vivid biblical imagery the meaning of the sacramental actions by which Christians take leave of their deceased. They serve well to guide the bereaved community step by step from the very time of death through burial itself and into future times of commemoration. The efforts of pastoral musicians to foster the singing of psalms, both through the necessary catechesis and through the composition of contemporary settings, are to be applauded and encouraged.

One cannot help but observe that these three successful lights in an otherwise musically drab funeral scene are becoming more and more familiar to Catholic people from their weekly celebrations of the Eucharist. This experience suggests a direction for solving the concern about teaching appropriate funeral music. Does not the weekly celebration of the paschal mystery itself offer the best opportunity for introducing new hymns, acclamations and psalms that can continue to enrich a parish repertoire of music equally appropriate for the funeral?

A particularly important element of the Rite of Funerals, highlighted in the MCW directive but scarcely sung at all in the United States, is the song of farewell. This situation perdures despite the many excellent compositions presently in circulation. It is attributable to a widespread misunderstanding of the rite of final commendation and farewell (frequently still considered a newly cast rite of purification) coupled with the fact that recited responses had become popular in the new American rite before the Rite of Funerals itself was published in English. In the spirit of the rite, however, the song of farewell is to be "experienced as the climax of the entire rite" of final commendation (*Rite of Funerals*, #10). It is to spell out in confident song, simple enough for all to sing, the community's final profession of faith and hope in paschal life untouched by physical death.

Although the song of farewell has remained virtually foreign to American funeral experience and the rite of final commendation itself is often a meaningless appendage to the funeral Mass, nevertheless the recessional song often serves the climactic function that the Rite assigns to the song of farewell. This is particularly the case when Suzanne Toolan's composition "I Am the Bread of Life" is sung during the procession with the body from the church. One cannot help but recognize here the birth in living liturgy of the kind of strong and effective song of farewell that Fred McManus called for a decade ago ("The Reformed Funeral Rite," *AER* 116 (1972), 133). Is the recessional being experienced by American Catholics as the fitting climax and most appropriate "song of farewell" at the funeral? If so, how can this liturgical experience best be integrated with the flow of the liturgy embodied in the Rite of Funerals?

Initial consideration of these questions suggests that such an effective song, so expressive of paschal faith, might take the present position of song of farewell, thus focusing attention on the climactic conclusion of the principal liturgy in the church rather than on the removal of the body. The natural flow of the funeral liturgy in the new rite takes the worship of the community in the church, especially the Eucharist, as its middle point. Everything else leads up to and flows away from that ecclesial center. The song of farewell is intended to bring the principal liturgy of the ecclesial community to a fitting close, whether this takes place after Mass in the church or later at the cemetery. For the recessional song to replace the song of farewell, understood in this way, seems to shift the emphasis away from such a climax and draw attention unduly to itself. In accordance with "The Liturgical Judgment," rather than changing the flow of the liturgy to accomodate a successful song, it would be preferable to use the successful song to allow the rite to serve the liturgy. In the case of Toolan's "I Am the Bread of Life," some pastoral musicians have used several verses as an appropriate song of farewell, followed by the concluding prayer of commendation, with the remainder of the piece serving as recessional song.

Returning to our first question—how is *Music in Catholic Worship* holding up today?—the "good news" deserves to be proclaimed. The principles and recommendations of this document continue to provide clear, if less than forceful, direction to the ongoing task of liturgical renewal. When studied with the Catholic funeral in mind, the document as a whole holds up quite well. Coupled with a renewed understanding of the Rite of Funerals itself, this document unquestionably contains an essential key to the clear liturgical expression of the paschal character of Christian death foreseen by the Vatican II *Constitution on the Liturgy.*

For this to happen, however, the renewed understanding of the Rite of Funerals is imperative. Essential to such a renewal is establishing the importance of viewing the Catholic funeral in its entirety. It is only there and in the broader pastoral context of care for the dying and for the bereaved after death that one can discern the nature of funeral liturgy.

The Rite of Funerals as a whole embraces wake, funeral Mass, final commendation-farewell and interment or cremation services. Prior to any practical considerations regarding music at these various liturgical moments stands the point of faith that this full funeral liturgy is a *celebration* of the *paschal mystery* of Christ. His death and resurrection alone give Christian meaning to the death of one of his faithful. Celebration of this mystery is what gathers the Christian community around a deceased sister or brother and his or her bereaved loved ones. Discerning moods of saddened grief and faith-filled joy as well as choosing appropriate music therefore must follow from an appreciation-in-faith of the paschal mystery and of the special meaning celebration has in Christian liturgy. In the present context one is reminded that no other liturgy tests the strength of this notion of celebration the way the funeral does. What else but faith in the mystery of Calvary touched by Easter would dare to call a funeral a "celebration"?

How does this principle help the pastoral musician? Above all, it alerts one to the expectation that the funeral as a whole (from wake to burial) is to be celebrated in the context of paschal faith. No part stands in isolation from the others. Whether at the funeral Mass or, when pastoral conditions permit, at the wake or cemetery services, one must strive to allow music to embody the full paschal mystery.

Attention to the grief process reveals that people express their loss differently at different times throughout the spread of funeral rites. Grief is not concentrated at any one moment, with the exception perhaps of burial itself. Thus, practically speaking, to look for distinct times to express grief (e.g., at the wake) and others to express paschal joy (e.g., at the funeral Mass) fails to take into account the special character of the Christian funeral. For neither grief nor joy taken separately is ever appropriate. The one returns us to medieval pessimism, and the other mirrors 20th-century escapism from the harsh reality of death. By the same token, musicians rightly insist that mixing, as it were, the emotions of grieving sorrow and Easter joy is musically impossible. To attempt to do so runs the risk of creating feelings of mournful resurrection or, even worse, glorious grief, as the composer Owen Alstott puts

An appreciation of the nature of funeral liturgy as a whole suggests a solution to this growing problem for pastoral musicians.

The Roman Catholic funeral is above all else a proclamation in word and sacrament that the Christ-life of the paschal mystery, begun with Christian initiation, not only does not end with human death but now for this deceased Christian finds completion in the eternal present beyond death. The solution to most appropriate music for Catholic funeral liturgy, therefore, can be sought in the composition and choice of both music and texts that express the *paschal faith. Hope* therefore, rather than either grief or joy is the predominant motif of the Rite of Funerals.

From the point of view of the funeral, music is after all not only "particularly important in the new burial rites"; it is normative. Not only are "the themes of hope and resurrection...very difficult to express" without music; they can only be expressed adequately in a liturgy in which music enjoys its rightful, integral place. Music alone enables the symbolism of funeral liturgy to express itself fully as worship.

Music in Catholic Worship: Section VII
CONCLUSION

CONCLUSION

84. There is a vital interest today in the Mass as prayer, and in this understanding of the Mass lies a principle of synthesis which is essential to good liturgical worship. When all strive with one accord to make the Mass a prayer, a sharing and celebration of Faith, the result is unity. Styles of music, choices of instruments, forms of celebration—all converge in a single purpose: that men and women of faith may proclaim and share that faith in prayer and Christ may grow among us all.

NOTES

1. Second Vatican Council, Constitution on the Liturgy (=CSL), No. 34.
2. Congregation of Rites, Instruction on Music in the Liturgy, March 5, 1967, no. 5e; *Roman Missal*, General Instruction (=GI), No. 73.
3. GI No. 313.
4. Bishops' Committee on the Liturgy (=BCL), April 18, 1966.
5. Congregation for Divine Worship (=CDW), Instruction on Mass for Special Gatherings, May 15, 1969.
6. BCL, February 17, 1967.
7. GI No. 1; cf. CSL No. 102.
8. Instruction on Music in the Liturgy, No. 11.
9. *Ibid.*, No. 8.
10. Cf. CSL, No. 112.
11. Cf. CSL, No. 114.
12. BCL, April 18, 1966.
13. National Conference of Catholic Bishops (=NCCB), November, 1967.
14. CSL, No. 121.
15. CSL, No. 28.
16. Instruction on Music in the Liturgy, No. 21.
17. BCL, April 18, 1966.
18. CSL, No. 114.
19. BCL, April 18, 1966.
20. Cf. CSL, No. 120; Instruction on Music in the Liturgy, Nos. 63–65; CDW Third Instruction, September 5, 1970, No. 3c.
21. NCCB, November 1967; cf. CSL No. 120.
22. GI, No. 8.
23. GI, No. 24.
24. Cf. *Roman Missal*, Blessing and Sprinkling of Holy Water, No. 1.
25. *Liturgy of the Hours*, General Instruction, Nos. 93–98.
26. GI, No. 54.
27. GI, No. 56.

28. GI, No. 57.
29. GI, No. 19, cf. Instruction on Music in the Liturgy, Nos. 28 and 36.
30. GI, No. 39.
31. GI, No. 56.
32. NCCB, November 1969.
33. *Ibid.*
34. NCCB, November 1968; cf. GI, No. 6
35. Cf. GI, No. 30.
36. GI, No. 31.
37. GI, No. 43.
38. NCCB, November 1967.
39. BCL, April 18, 1966.
40. BCL, April 1969.
41. Cf. CSL, No. 27.
42. Rite of Baptism for Children, No. 5: 32 and 35.
43. Rite of Funerals, Introduction, No. 4.

THE PASTORAL PRESS

The following books are among those available from The Pastoral Press, 225 Sheridan Street, NW, Washington, DC 20011, (202) 723-5800.

THE MYSTERY OF FAITH: **THE MINISTERS OF MUSIC** by Lawrence J. Johnson. The most inclusive presentation of the new ministries of music since Vatican II. Provides a first-time history of the ministries of music complete with documentation. Easy to read follow-up for parishes that used THE MYSTERY OF FAITH study (FDLC). Includes special treatment of liturgical composer and deacon. $5.95

LYRIC PSALMS: HALF A PSALTER by Francis Patrick Sullivan. A major breakthrough in psalm prayer. Takes the best scholarship on the psalms and adds a new poetic effort. Beautiful blend of ancient and contemporary prayer. Inclusive poetry that gives new breath to all who pray. An excellent gift. $5.95

MUSIC & WORSHIP IN PAGAN & CHRISTIAN ANTIQUITY by Johannes Quasten. Translation by Boniface Ramsey. Long awaited translation of revised German text. Single source for information about liturgy and music in patristic period. Special feature: Liturgical singing of women in the early church—Why its decline? $10.95

TO GIVE THANKS AND PRAISE: GENERAL INSTRUCTION OF THE ROMAN MISSAL WITH COMMENTARY FOR MUSICIANS AND PRIESTS by Ralph A. Keifer. Provides access to the General Instruction for everyone, not just clergy. Practical combination of official liturgical rules and the best commentary for liturgy planners. Handy reference tool of celebration suggestions for clergy. $4.95

PROPHECIES AND PUZZLES: A SEVEN DAY RETREAT FOR THOSE IN MUSIC MINISTRY by Cynthia Serjak. Do-it-yourself retreat for individual pastoral musicians and/or groups. Each day's journey contains scripture reflection, suggested music for listening, playing, meditation, and closing prayer. Combines serious reflection with humor. $6.95

For complete catalogue of books available from The Pastoral Press, please write to above address.